Contemporary Irish Masculinities

By examining portrayals of male homosociality in Sally Rooney's novels, the book documents how male relationships are formed, challenged, and often disavowed and the profound negative effects this can have for the well-being of men. The book also highlights the importance of the sociocultural context within which male relationships are formed and supports that the potential for healthy and meaningful relationships between men depends on how they are brought up to view themselves as men and their role in the society they live in. That is, despite the many examples whereby space for authentic and meaningful male homosociality is limited and well concealed, the book also offers a more optimistic potential for men's relationships by illustrating the significance of broader understandings of masculinity, unfettered by homophobia and misogyny, in allowing for male homosociality with the potential of emancipating men from heteropatriarchal norms which dictate their behaviour toward themselves and others.

Angelos Bollas is Assistant Professor in the School of Communications at Dublin City University. His research focuses on masculinity and sexuality studies. He writes about cultural representations of masculinities in television and literature, expressions of masculinities which challenge normative understandings of gender and sexuality, as well as pedagogical considerations around inclusion and diversity.

For more information about this series, please visit: www.routledge.com/Routledge-Focus-on-Literature/book-series/RFLT

Contemporary Irish Masculinities

Male Homosociality in Sally Rooney's Novels

Angelos Bollas

Routledge
Taylor & Francis Group

NEW YORK AND LONDON

First published 2024
by Routledge
605 Third Avenue, New York, NY 10158

and by Routledge
4 Park Square, Milton Park, Abingdon, Oxon, OX14 4RN

Routledge is an imprint of the Taylor & Francis Group, an informa business

© 2024 Angelos Bollas

ISBN: 978-1-032-64490-5 (hbk)
ISBN: 978-1-032-64496-7 (pbk)
ISBN: 978-1-032-64497-4 (ebk)

DOI: 10.4324/9781032644974

Typeset in Times New Roman
by Apex CoVantage, LLC

Contents

Acknowledgements

I would like to thank Dr Deirdre Flynn for her academic and intellectual generosity, her always insightful suggestions, her encouragement, and the kindness with which she approached this work.

I would also like to thank Eugene Ryan and April Quin for reading a draft version of this book and sharing valuable feedback with me, Jennifer Abbott for believing and supporting this book, and Gerasimos Evangelatos for reminding me that it is in books where we can find ourselves when everything else fails.

I do not have the right words to explain the pivotal role Dr Anastasia Logotheti has played in my intellectual life. My most sincere gratitude goes to her for having been the teacher I will always aspire to be.

This book would not have been written had it not been for the patience and understanding of my partner who gave me time and space to think and write. This is only one of the many reasons to be grateful for him.

Finally, this book is dedicated to my chosen family whose presence in my life has been a true gift.

Introduction

One of the first examinations of male homosociality, the nonsexual and non-romantic relationships between men, that popularised the concept in academic discourse (Sedgwick, 1985) as well as many that followed (e.g. Bird, 1996) focused a lot on understanding homosociality as an enabler of patriarchy and hegemonic masculinity, as a regulating social mechanism that ensures the prevalence of misogyny and homophobia without compromising men's need to feel and express desire for other men. This is particularly pronounced in Sedgwick's work (1985, pp. 1–5) where a triangular structure is introduced to provide a visualisation of male homosociality. In an oversimplified manner, this triangle involves two men and one woman. The two men feel a strong (non-sexual) desire toward each other, but this can only be expressed, materialised, or realised through the woman (with whom sexual desire is allowed). As such, this structure illustrates the policing of homosexual desire and the subservient role of women, both of which aid in the maintenance of patriarchy. The function of homosociality in separating men from women is also highlighted by Lipman-Blumen (1976), who offers the first theorisation of male homosociality. However, Bird (1996, pp. 130–131) examines male homosociality with attention to highlighting its structural foundations which promote a hierarchical arrangement of men on the basis of their adherence to heteropatriarchal rules. These, according to Bird (1996, p. 121), are: being emotionally distant, having a strong desire for competition, and devaluing women by viewing them primarily as sexual objects. Additionally, Bird (1996, pp. 130–131) explains that homosocial relationships between men are structured in such a closely regulated manner that make those who do not abide by these rules be relegated to an inferior role in the hierarchical ladder of masculinity. Examining male homosociality as a mechanism that promotes hegemonic heteropatriarchal ideals has been fruitful to a certain extent, mainly in that it has allowed for an understanding of the role of social relationships in establishing and promoting societal segregation on the basis of gender and gendered behaviour. However, such a perspective is limited in that it presents the dynamics of male homosocial relationships as static and transhistorical. In other words, examining

DOI: 10.4324/9781032644974-1

male homosociality merely as an instrument of heteropatriarchy provides no possibilities for change, let alone transgression, and presents women and men who do not conform to patriarchal and/or hegemonic versions of masculinity as *a priori* victims of an invisible force. That is not to ignore or diminish the pervasiveness of heteropatriarchy; rather, such a criticism calls into attention the potential for change that is inherent in any binary relationship – men-women, heterosexual-homosexual – whereby, irrespective of the asymmetrical allocation of power, the seemingly powerless are never completely powerless. Without challenging these earlier conceptualisations of male homosociality, it is important to consider these social relationships in a more nuanced manner, examining not only how they promote a certain social order but also how such a social order is shaping and regulating the ways these social relationships are to be formed and experienced, as well as how changing and emerging understandings of gender and sexuality can challenge the ways in which such social relationships are organised and structured.

Recent studies of male homosociality offer more complex analyses reflecting a gradual change in the ways in which such relationships are organised. Haywood *et al.* (2018, p. 56) also observe that descriptive explanations of male homosociality might be important in that they illustrate how 'men, through their friendships and intimate collaborations with other men, maintain and defend the gender order and patriarchy'. However, they argue, such examinations of male homosociality fall short of recording 'contradictory and ambivalent aspects of homosociality', referring to the potential of male-to-male relationships to both uphold and subvert established norms around masculinity and patriarchy. This follows from recent theorisations within masculinity studies which observe a changing pattern in the way masculinities, in the plural, are understood, assumed, and expressed by men, a pattern that reflects a diversion from the earlier hegemonic masculinity model whereby power-related categories were fixed and one-dimensional (Anderson, 2009; Buschmeyer and Lengersdorf, 2016, pp. 202–203; Messerschmidt, 2018, p. 142). Such analytical understandings of masculinities have also resulted in analyses of male homosociality that focus on how men's relationships with other men are shaped and restricted by heteropatriarchal norms (e.g. Pascoe, 2007) as well as examinations of the subversive potential of male homosociality with regard to challenging traditional understandings of and norms about masculinity (e.g. Robinson and Anderson, 2022). By focusing on literary representations of male homosociality, the present book illustrates male characters' inability to form meaningful relationships with other male characters as a result of societal restrictions around public displays of masculinity, and it further focuses on rarer instances of non-restrictive male homosociality which appear to be allowed to emerge on the proviso that they remain invisible to the public eye. In doing so, the book locates male homosociality as a site of learned gendered behaviour and a site of struggle where men, and particularly young boys, are tasked with concealing their vulnerabilities, needs for emotional expression, and, in turn, their authentic selves.

By examining portrayals of male homosociality, the book documents how male relationships are formed, challenged, and often disavowed as well as the profound negative effects this can have for the well-being of the male characters in the novels in focus. At the same time, the book highlights the importance of the sociocultural context within which male relationships are to be formed and supports that the potential for healthy and meaningful relationships between men exists and lies with how men are brought up to view themselves as men and their role in the society and culture they live in. That is, despite the many examples whereby space for authentic and meaningful male homosociality is limited and well concealed, the last chapter of the book also offers a more optimistic potential for men's relationships by illustrating the significance of broader understandings of masculinity, unfettered by homophobia and misogyny, in allowing for male homosociality with the potential of emancipating men from heteropatriarchal norms which dictate their behaviour toward themselves and others. What is meant by 'authentic' and 'healthy' with reference to male homosociality is discussed in detail in the chapters that follow, but in short, these refer to relationships between men whereby men bond with each other on the basis of their own emotional needs without any pretext, such as homophobia or misogyny; that is, men connecting with one another not on the basis of their shared negative attitudes toward gay men or women, among others, but on the basis of who they are, what they need, and what they feel.

The source material for this study are the works of Sally Rooney. Her works were selected not only for the profound success they have had (Grady, 2019; Sweeney, 2021) but primarily because they are set in the contemporary Irish context which, given the changes it is undergoing, provides significant opportunities for sociological explorations of any kind. Sell (2023) and Darling (2023) describe Rooney, among others, as a Celtic Phoenix writer, situating her work in the post-Celtic-Tiger era where financial institutions, and the societal structures that come with or are affected by them, have collapsed, leaving Irish society, in all its tragedy, in the unique position where it can rebuild and redefine itself. That is, along with the economy, all aspects of society, including masculinity and gender-related issues, can be rediscovered and renegotiated. Indeed, Darcy's (2019, pp. 29–30) research confirms a change in the way Irish men understand, express, and perform masculinity with attention to a mostly conscious disavowal of traditional models of masculinity and an adoption of more flexible ways of expressing masculine gender identity. Even though the study does not focus in detail on how this change affects the ways in which men relate to other men, Darcy (2019) indicates that through male homosociality, young Irish men attempt to redefine new Irish masculinities as well as their place within this new, emerging understanding. An additional reason for choosing Rooney's works in this exploration of male homosociality, which might appear odd, is a contradiction. A distinguishing feature of her fiction is her perceptive narration of contemporary female consciousness, and, as such, male characters might appear as secondary. However, as the discussion in the chapters that follow demonstrate, the male characters in her work are crafted with nuance and depth, suggesting that it might not be female consciousness that Rooney focuses on, but heteropatriarchy and its effects on her female as well as male characters. Further to this, the male characters in Rooney's works span across a range of socioeconomic backgrounds, allowing for more intersectional examinations whereby gendered behaviour might be affected by aspects such as social class, wealth, and fame. In a sense, such range of male characters that are included in Rooney's work provide opportunities for a review of a number of possible male homosocial configurations. The only exception to this is male characters who come from less privileged backgrounds as they are not portrayed in Rooney's novels. Indeed, the novels include some male characters from a working-class background, such as Connell from *Normal People*, though even them find themselves in a privileged position. In the case of Connell, for instance, he can afford to attend Trinity College in Dublin to study English, even if under scholarship, and pursue his passion for literature and, as it becomes later known, for writing. Felix from *Beautiful World, Where Are You* is perhaps a more representative example of a male character from a working-class background whose career and life trajectories have been affected by his socioeconomic standing significantly more than Connell's. As such, the range of male characters as well as the setting of the novels in a contemporary society that has very recently undergone significant changes contribute to making these works appropriate source material for a study on male homosociality, which, as the following chapters suggest, is itself undergoing significant changes.

The use of literature, instead of empirical data collection methods, to discuss a topic such as male homosociality situates this book within the long-standing tradition of sociological readings of literature which are based on the contention that fiction contains ideological information that readers are inevitably involved with every time they engage with the work of fiction itself (Hollindale, 1998, p. 22). Such readings are further based on the contention that works of literature illustrate social structures and processes that not only reflect the social milieu of their times but can also be used as blueprints for (re)organising and (re)defining their societies (de Certeau, 1984, pp. 166–174; Ewick and Silbey, 1998, p. 220; Singer, 2011, pp. 314–315). It follows that works of fiction can indeed provide useful opportunities for analyses of social issues with attention to how these contribute to the experiences and behaviours of literary characters. In this way, sociological analyses of fiction are able to complement, illustrate, and problematise empirical and theoretical analyses of sociological phenomena, especially when works of fiction are viewed as both products and producers of societal and cultural processes. By this, I refer to fiction as both emerging from, and thus mirroring, as well as promoting specific sociocultural conditions and structures. The novel, in particular, has long been used as a significant contributor to various national projects of building and cementing national identity (Franssen and Kuipers, 2015, p. 291). A consideration of the importance parents, academics, and political groups place on which literary books people, especially kids, read – or are allowed to read – illustrates the significance of works of fiction and their contribution to establishing social norms. It is for these reasons that the present book uses works of fiction to explore male homosociality. In particular, the book analyses all instances of interaction between and among male characters in Rooney's works with attention to how these are shaped by the sociocultural context within which they occur as well as to the potential they might offer to readers for a reconceptualisation of relationships between men and the possibility of such reconceptualisation to challenge established heteropatriarchal norms about masculinities and accepted masculine behaviour. The book does not discuss the presentation of contemporary Irish masculinities in general or in relation to Ireland's project of modernity; I have done this elsewhere (Bollas, 2022). Rather, it focuses solely on exploring how men engage, if at all, with other men and how such relationships are formed within and encouraged or discouraged by the socioeconomic and cultural conditions of each male character as well as contemporary Irish society. It is hoped that the book will contribute to the broader field of masculinity studies in that it challenges the concept of male homosociality by asking whether it is even possible for men to engage with other men in a meaningful, honest, and unrestrictive manner.

Overview of the Book

In Sally Rooney's novels, the absence of meaningful relationships among men paints a picture of a world where same-sex friendships are rare. This phenomenon of impossible homosociality is introduced in the first chapter, which delves into the complex ways masculine gender expression is shaped and reshaped through interactions among men. Focusing primarily on Nick's interactions with other men in *Conversations with Friends*, Chapter 1 analyses instances where men share the same space but rarely, if at all, engage with each other. By examining similar instances in Rooney's other novels, *Normal People* and *Beautiful World, Where Are You*, the argument is put forth that men hinder their own potential for homosociality by repressing admiration, participating in trivial relationships, and resorting to public displays of belittlement. The rigid adherence to societal scripts of masculinity becomes a barrier preventing men from forming meaningful bonds with one another. Through an exploration of these dynamics, Rooney's work sheds light on the complexities of male relationships and the challenges they face in fostering meaningful connections. Building upon the first chapter and its examination of hollow relationships among men in *Conversations with Friends*, and the concept of impossible male homosociality, the second chapter demonstrates how teenage boys learn to conform to societal gendered scripts, leading to isolation and the challenge of establishing meaningful bonds. Focusing on *Normal People* and Connell's adolescent years and his interactions with fellow teenage boys in high school, the second chapter analyses how teenage boys negotiate and define male homosociality during this developmental stage. Through an examination of male-to-male interactions, the intricate relationship among hegemony, masculinities, and homosociality is focused on. Additionally, Chapter 2 highlights the significance of sports-related contexts as safe spaces that allow for public displays of emotional connections among men and teenage boys, underscoring the often-unacknowledged importance of intimacy for men. The third chapter also analyses male homosocial relationships in *Normal People*, with a particular focus on the characters' adult years during their time at university. By shifting the focus to adulthood, a more nuanced exploration unfolds, revealing how homosocial relationships intersect with social inequalities and gendered hierarchies. Chapter 3 begins by addressing the influence of social class and socioeconomic status in shaping the dynamics of these relationships. It then delves into the potential positive aspects of homosociality for young men, highlighting its benefits for mental and emotional well-being. Furthermore, Chapter 3 considers the notion that male homosocial relationships are more acceptable when they remain invisible or hidden. The central argument of the chapter asserts that societal norms surrounding masculinity mandate public displays of conflicting homosociality, where men assert dominance over each other, while public expressions of affectionate homosociality are discouraged or limited, regardless of whether they occur privately. By exploring these dynamics, Chapter 3 sheds light on the complexities of male homosocial relationships and the societal expectations that shape them. The final chapter focuses on Rooney's novel *Beautiful World, Where Are You*, which delves into the intricacies of men's homosocial relationships, offering a closer exploration of how these dynamics are formed and what their significance is. Unlike her previous works, this book dedicates ample time and space to examine the possibility of homosociality between Felix and Simon. It highlights the need for such relationships and the benefits they offer, presenting an optimistic outlook on contemporary masculinities. This last chapter begins by discussing the lack of emotional fluency in brother-brother and father-son relationships, asserting the relevance of these familial relationships in analysing male homosociality. Further, it explores the relationship between Felix and Simon as the only positive and discernible example of male homosociality in Rooney's novels. Utilising inclusive masculinity theory, Chapter 4 examines the sociocultural conditions that foster such connections and their potential positive impact.

References

Anderson, E. (2009) *Inclusive masculinities: The changing nature of masculinity*. London: Routledge.

Bird, S. R. (1996) 'Welcome to the men's club: Homosociality and the maintenance of hegemonic masculinity', *Gender & Society*, 10(2), pp. 120–132. https://doi.org/10.1177/089124396010002002.

Bollas, A. (2022) 'Normal people (2020) and the new post-Celtic Irish man', *Journal of Popular Film and Television*, 50(2), pp. 50–59. https://doi.org/10.1080/01956051.20 22.2033156.

Buschmeyer, A. and Lengersdorf, D. (2016) 'The differentiation of masculinity as a challenge for the concept of hegemonic masculinity', *NORMA*, 11(3), pp. 190–207. https:// doi.org/10.1080/18902138.2016.1217672.

Darcy, C. J. (2019) '"We don't really give a fiddlers about anything": The ambiguity, contradiction and fluidity of Irish masculinities', *Irish Journal of Applied Social Studies*, 19(1), pp. 16–32. https://doi.org/10.21427/aa58-qr67.

Darling, O. (2023) 'The Celtic phoenix, capitalist realism, and contemporary Irish women's novels', *Irish Studies Review*, 31(3), pp. 348–362. https://doi.org/10.1080/09670882. 2023.2233324.

de Certeau, M. (1984) *The practice of everyday life*. Berkeley: University of California Press.

Ewick, P. and Silbey, S. S. (1998) *The common place of law: Stories from everyday life*. Chicago: University of Chicago Press.

Franssen, T. and Kuipers, G. (2015) 'Sociology of literature and publishing in the early 21st century: Away from the centre', *Cultural Sociology*, 9(3), pp. 291–295. https:// doi.org/10.1177/1749975515594467.

Grady, C. (2019) 'The cult of Sally Rooney: How reading Sally Rooney became a status symbol', *Vox*, 3 September. Available at: https://www.vox.com/culture/2019/9/3/20807728/ sally-rooney-normal-people-conversations-with-friends (Accessed: 30 May 2023).

Haywood, C., Johansson, T., Hammarén, N., Marcus, H. and Ottemo, A. (2018) *The conundrum of masculinity: Hegemony, homosociality, homophobia, and heteronormativity*. New York: Routledge.

Hollindale, P. (1998) *Ideology and the children's book*. Gloucestershire: Thimble Press.

Lipman-Blumen, J. (1976) 'Toward a homosocial theory of sex roles: An explanation of the sex segregation of social institutions', *Signs*, 1(3), pp. 15–31. https://www.jstor. org/stable/3172990.

Messerschmidt, J. W. (2018) *Hegemonic masculinity: Formulation, reformulation, and amplification*. London: Rowman & Littlefield.

Pascoe, C. J. (2007) *Dude, you're a fag: Masculinity and sexuality in high school*. Berkeley: University of California Press.

Robinson, S. and Anderson, E. (2022) *Bromance: Male friendship, love and sport*. Basingstoke: Palgrave Macmillan.

Sedgwick, E. K. (1985) *Between men: English literature and male homosocial desire*. New York: Columbia University Press.

Sell, A. W. (2023) 'Even better than the real thing: A conceptual history of the "Celtic phoenix"', *Irish Studies Review*, 31(3), pp. 331–347. https://doi.org/10.1080/09670882. 2023.2233325.

Singer, A. E. (2011) 'A novel approach: The sociology of literature, children's books, and social inequality', *International Journal of Qualitative Methods*, 10(4), pp. 307–320. https://doi.org/10.1177/160940691101000401.

Sweeney, T. (2021) 'The Sally Rooney effect: How the runaway success of normal people sparked a fresh publishing phenomenon', *Independent.ie*, 30 April. Available at: https:// www.independent.ie/entertainment/books/the-sally-rooney-effect-how-the-runaway-success-of-normal-people-sparked-a-fresh-publishing-phenomenon/40372078.html (Accessed: 30 June 2023).

1 Impossible Male Homosociality

Relationships among men in the novels of Sally Rooney are few and far between, presenting a world where men do not engage in same-sex friendships. As the introduction to this book demonstrates, homosociality has monopolised scholarly interest in light of its contribution toward the maintenance of hegemonic forms of masculinities as well as its possibilities for subverting these very forms and signifying a turn toward what Anderson (2009, p. 31), among others, discusses as inclusive masculinities. In Sally Rooney's novels, men do not act in a homogeneous manner. Rather, different ways in which homosociality is manifested are presented, allowing for examination of the complex ways in which masculine gender expression is both formed and reformed as a result of men's interactions with other men. This chapter examines the rather limited instances of homosociality primarily in *Conversations with Friends* through Nick's interactions with other men, or lack thereof, though it also provides examples from the other two novels by Sally Rooney. What is presented in this chapter is a close reading of all the instances where Nick finds himself in the same space as other men, whether they engage in any form of interaction or not. The chapter draws on similar instances that are found in Rooney's two other novels, *Normal People* and *Beautiful World, Where Are You*, to put forward the argument that by repressing their admiration toward one another, by participating in insignificant relationships with one another, and by engaging in public expressions of belittling one another, men can find themselves in situations where homosociality becomes impossible for them. Rigid adherence to social scripts of masculinity can become an obstacle for men to form serious and meaningful bonds with other men.

As a result of regulated masculine behaviour with regard to the limitations around the extent to and the ways in which a man's admiration toward another man is to be expressed, instances of male homosocial relations in Rooney's novels are observed to be limited. That is, even though admiration is not the foundation of homosociality, avoiding expressing appreciation for another man can lead to avoidance of engagement in any possible homosocial relationship. One day, Frances offers Philip, her co-worker, a ticket to a theatre performance where Nick would be the main actor. Frances explains that 'Philip kept asking

DOI: 10.4324/9781032644974-2

if we [Philip and Frances] were going to have to talk to Nick afterwards, and I didn't know. . . . Philip had never met Nick but had seen him on TV and considered his looks "intimidating"' (CWF, p. 28, emphasis in original). It appears that Philip admires Nick by his insistence to meet him after the play. His admiration for Nick's physical appearance is further highlighted when Philip and Frances arrive at the theatre, and after buying the programme, he 'leafed straight to the actor bios and showed me [Frances] Nick's photograph. In the dim light it was really just an outline of a face. Look at his jaw, he said' (CWF, p. 28). After the end of the play, the discussion between Philip and Frances is almost exclusively focused on Nick's appearance again, with Frances acknowledging how handsome Nick is and Philip responding that he is so handsome '[t]o an almost off-putting extent' (CWF, p. 29). Two nights later, Philip meets Nick at a club where Bobbi and Frances are giving one of their spoken word performances. After the end of the performance, Melissa and Nick invite Bobbi, Frances, and Philip to join them at their table. Despite Philip's admiration for Nick, when Bobbi introduces them at the club, Philip's appears to be reserved, hiding any feelings of appreciation, let alone adoration, he might have for Nick. He 'congratulated Nick on the play and they talked about Tennessee Williams' (CWF, p. 37). It appears that during the rest of the night, the two men do not engage in conversation with one another. Even though at that point in the novel Philip's sexuality is not presented, later in the novel he dates a girl which suggests that he is either bisexual or heterosexual. In either case, it is clear from the minimal exchanges they have that any interest or admiration one man has toward another cannot be declared. Badin (2016, p. 115), in his analysis of homosociality in the novel of Rachid O, *Plusieurs Vies* (1996), observes a very similar pattern whereby the young male narrator of the novel experiences a strong physical attraction toward his uncle (not a biological one, as it transpires later on in the novel); however, this desire is not expressed for a significant part of the novel as a result of the two men following a social script that dictates what types of homosocial exchanges are allowed between men. Similar arguments have been put forward by Ibson (2002) who observes men's reluctance to explicitly express their admiration for one another, in public or private, as a form of self-policing one's gender expression. The extracts from *Conversations with Friends* discussed earlier highlight the contradiction between Philip's excitement with Nick's physical presence and his demeanour when he finally meets him, supporting the importance of distance in one's manifestation of masculinity.

Even when the five of them step out of the club to smoke, their interactions are minimal. Nick is acting in a reserved manner toward Frances because, as he admits later, Philip is there. When Philip visits the toilets, Frances tells us that Nick 'had waited for Philip to leave us [Frances and Nick] alone so he [Nick] could address this sentence to me [Frances]' (CWF, p. 38). The sentence refers to Nick's apology to Frances for being late and missing her spoken word performance. Indeed, this is the first time in the novel where two men are in the company of each other, and their interactions are very limited. On the one hand, Philip does not express his excitement for meeting Nick, though this could be explained partially by the fact that Nick is a local celebrity and Philip might be intimidated by this in addition to him monitoring his gender expression in public. On the other hand, Nick does not only appear disinterested in having a chat with Philip, but he also appears to be limiting his interactions with Frances while Philip is present, as if he cannot engage in a meaningful conversation with her while another man is present. It could be argued that this is linked to an attempt to hide adulterous desire; however, later in the novel it transpires that Nick does not actively try to hide his desire for Frances. Mair Underwood's study in 2018 exploring digital homosociality confirms that men are less likely to express emotions not only toward one another but also toward a woman, be it their romantic/sexual partner or a stranger, when they find themselves in physical proximity with one another (Underwood, 2018, p. 161). The study further shows that when the same men interact with other men and women in the digital world, they are less likely to show signs of emotional detachment. Notwithstanding the opportunities the digital world affords to male homosociality, it is important to note that emotional detachment – something that is further discussed in this chapter – is one of the primary characteristics of male homosociality (Bird, 1996, pp. 125–127), and the way the two men behave in the scene discussed earlier attests to this. The remaining interactions Nick has with other men in *Conversations with Friends*, as well as the ones peripheral male characters in the other novels of Sally Rooney engage in, show a pattern of organisation of homosociality that is based on insignificant bonds and interactions as well as public performances of disrespect and belittlement.

In the scene where Dennis, Frances' father, takes Frances to the local pub for dinner, the other men in the pub are very complementary of Frances and her progress. However, they direct these complements to her father, Dennis, rather than directly at her, suggesting that she is somehow not only his creation but his possession, and, therefore, any credit about herself is to be given to him. '[W]hen we went to McCarthy's in the afternoons, my father's friends would ask: this is your little prodigy, is it, Dennis?' (CWF, p. 50). Given that Frances' parents were separated while she was still in school and the many problems he has had with alcohol and – possibly – gambling, his pub friends will be aware that he has been absent for most of Frances' life. However, not only is there no acknowledgement of this but they are complementary toward him for the achievements of his daughter. Even though this is an example of a positive exchange among men who praise one another, it is rather telling of their inability to engage in any honest or meaningful conversation with each other. They could, for example, acknowledge Frances' achievements and complement her, while reprimanding Dennis for being an absentee father figure to her, let alone his violent behaviour toward her when she was younger. What is interesting about this exchange is that instead of receiving compliments from her father, Frances is complimented by his father's friends. On the one hand, it appears that Dennis is very proud of her since he has shared her accomplishments with his friends. However, this scene illustrates Dennis's inability to venture outside the role he has for himself and show pride in his daughter directly. Instead, he uses his male circle to indirectly compliment her.

Additionally, in the very few instances where men engage in any kind of interaction in the novel, what they say to one another appears to be insignificant. For example, when Nick's sister, Laura, and his brother-in-law, Jim, are at Nick's birthday party, the narrator describes Jim and Nick talking to each other but cannot remember the contents of their conversation. 'Laura handed me the baby and said she was going to get herself a glass of soda water. Jim and Nick were talking about something, I don't remember what' (CWF, p. 281). Arguably, this could be explained by the fact that Frances is under stress expecting Bobbi to appear at the party despite having fallen out over the essay Frances published about Bobbi without telling her. She could have been overwhelmed by having been confronted by Melissa about her affair with Nick or by getting to meet his relatives. Even so, the insignificance of the conversation that Jim and Nick have at that time is logged in the narrative, allowing readers to further reflect on the very limited, and arguably meaningless, opportunities for connection afforded to men.

In a classic empirical study of same- and cross-sex friendships among 90 young adults in the Pittsburgh area, Rose (1985, p. 68) demonstrates that men are less likely to engage in homosocial relations because their kinship needs are often fulfilled through their cross-sex friendships and romantic relations. Therefore, despite the scholarly attention on homosociality, much of which is presented in the introductory chapter of this book, and without moderating the significance of homosocial relations in both maintaining (e.g. Bird, 1996, pp. 130–131; Flood, 2008, p. 355; Gilmartin, 2007, pp. 537–538) and challenging male privilege (e.g. Anderson, 2008, p. 608, 2009, pp. 151–152; Hammarén and Johansson, 2014, pp. 7–9), it is important to consider men's reluctance to form meaningful connections with other men and its significance. It follows that this impossibility of male homosociality is not observed only in Rooney's novels, but it is manifested in the day-to-day experiences of men. None of the instances discussed earlier portray men forming meaningful bonds with other men. Neither the relationship among Frances' father, Dennis, with his friends nor Nick's relationship with Jim appear to be ones where 'acceptance, loyalty, help, intimacy, [or] companionship' (Rose, 1985, p. 71) are manifested. Many psychology studies confirm heterosexual men's disinclination to form intimate relations with other men (e.g. Bell, 1981, p. 402; Fischer and Narus, 1981, p. 444; Caldwell and Peplau, 1982, p. 731). Rose (1985, p. 73) argues that this is less frequently the case with married heterosexual men because, as the findings of her study suggest, men report stronger desire for same-sex relationships possibly because they are no longer in competition with one another over finding suitable female romantic and/or sexual partners. This claim does not shed light on Nick's very few male-to-male relationships; there are no indications as to whether he has any desire to have more such relationships or whether the fact that he does not have meaningful relations with other men affects him in any way.

Lack of male homosociality is not limited to *Conversations with Friends*. In Rooney's novels, men appear to be avoiding interacting with one another. When, in *Normal People*, Connell, Elaine, and Niall are on their trip around Europe by train, Connell and Niall do not exchange a single word. We are told that they spend a lot of time in the train carriage and in various European cities, and that they have plans for a few more city breaks before they would arrive in Italy to see Marianne and her friends, but throughout all this journey, there is not a single interaction narrated between Connell and Niall (NP, pp. 153–160). This is rather surprising given that the two men are housemates in Dublin, and they seem to have a very good relationship. Similarly, in *Beautiful World, Where Are You*, men also appear to have very limited interactions with one another. For example, in the scene where Simon and Eileen are at Leanne's party, Simon engages in conversation primarily with Leanne and some other women that are there, but he never talks to any of his male friends. 'While Eileen listened [to an anecdote someone was sharing], her eyes travelled back to the kitchen doorway, through which Simon's figure was still partly visible. Following her gaze, Peter said: The big man. I didn't know he was here' (BWWAY, p. 198). Peter's remark suggests that not only do the two men know each other but they appear to be more than acquaintances. Despite this, though, he says that he did not know Simon would be there, suggesting that not only did he not seek out any of his male friends when he arrived at the party but, even prior to that, their communication must have been so limited that Simon had not mentioned that he would be there. Also, the next night, when Alice goes to a pub to meet Felix and his friends, the novel does not include any interaction between Felix and his friends except when he addresses Alice and tells her that she already knows them. 'Gesturing back at his friends, he added: you know? them? crowd, you've met them before' (BWWAY, p. 214). The remaining part of the narration focuses exclusively on the interactions between Felix and Alice, with some interjections about a story one of Felix's female friends was sharing.

Even when opportunities for more meaningful communication arise, it appears that the men in Rooney's novels decide not to engage in such, possibly so that frictions do not arise. For example, in *Conversations with Friends*, when Melissa, Nick, and their friends were having dinner in Étables, they start talking about the refugee crisis in Europe, with Bobbi and Derek engaging in a heated argument over 'Western value systems' and '[t]he naive dream of multiculturalism' (CWF, p. 112). At no moment does Nick participate in the argument except to laugh at one of Bobbi's sarcastic comments toward Derek and, a few moments later, to respond to Derek's plea for support.

> Nick, you're an oppressive white male, you back me up [said Derek]. I actually agree with Bobbi, said Nick. Oppressive though I certainly am. Oh, God

save us, Derek said. Who needs liberal democracy? Maybe we should just burn down Government Buildings and see where that gets us. I know you're exaggerating, said Nick, but increasingly it's hard to see why not.

(CWF, p. 112)

Derek's expectation that Nick would support him appears to be based solely on the fact that Nick is another man, and, therefore, his being a man would, in some way, qualify a concert of opinion between the two. To Derek's surprise, Nick, while acknowledging his white male privilege, assumes a more radical stance. Even though this is not a stance that is reflected in Nick's lifestyle in any way, his comment challenges not only Derek's political position but, most importantly, his assumption that as men they would share similar viewpoints. In a sense, for Derek, manhood appears to signify not only a reason for kinship but also a signifier of an affinity among men.

A similar attitude to Derek's is observed at a later scene in the novel when Frances and Bobbie meet their friends Andrew, Marianne, Philip, and Camille for coffee after Frances hands in one of her essays. The group starts discussing monogamy and sexuality, and very quickly Bobbi dominates that conversation, steering it toward a more abstract theoretical discourse which is not perceived positively by the rest of the group:

I noticed that Philip and Camille were exchanging glances. At one point Philip looked at Andrew, the only other man seated with us, and Andrew raised both his eyebrows as if Bobbi had started talking gibberish or promoting anti-Semitism. I thought it was cowardly of Philip to look at Andrew, whom I knew he didn't even like, and it made me uncomfortable.

(CWF, p. 253)

Similar to Derek's behaviour that was analysed earlier, the two men here are looking for each other's support regarding their sentiment toward Bobbi's enthusiasm, despite the fact that neither are they close friends, nor do they like one another. Once again, it appears that their being men qualifies adequately their expectation of having a shared reaction toward a particular situation.

Male homosociality in Sally Rooney's novels appears to be based on men engaging in insignificant exchanges as well as on their ability to belittle each other publicly. In a very rare scene where Nick appears in the company of his male friends, their relationship seems to be reduced to them embarrassing him in front of others. Specifically, at Melissa's birthday party, Frances finds Nick in the utility room with four more people smoking pot and getting drunk. None of them know who Frances is or whether she is Nick's friend. Despite this, one of his friends asks her whether she is 'another actress' (CWF, p. 55) without making it clear whether he means another actress that Nick is attracted to or just another actress in the house. Another friend continues, saying that 'Nick has to be careful where he looks' (CWF, p. 56), referring to the short cut of Frances' dress. While narrating this, Frances acknowledges that the comments Nick's friends make have a sexual connotation. 'I knew at this point that I was being interpreted as some kind of vaguely disruptive sexual presence for the sake of their joke' (CWF, p. 56). Even though the exchange focuses on Frances' presence, this is an example of a superficiality in the relationship men have with other men, which appears to be based around sexual prowess and the notion that men cannot control their sexual desires. Especially as this is a rare example of interactions among men, and taking into consideration Nick's unsurprised reaction to this, it could be understood as a typical example of how Nick and his friends interact with each other, not only in terms of the manner that they talk about one another but also with attention to the content of their exchanges. His friends' comments are focused on Frances' appearance, suggesting the possibility of sexual attraction between her and Nick without leaving room for the possibility of any deeper feelings between the two, as if Nick is unable to have feelings for another person or, quite possibly, as if his feelings are a private concern of his alone. The superficial nature of their relationship is further highlighted later in a scene that depicts an exchange that initially appears to be demeaning toward Frances but actually constitutes an attempt to belittle Nick. Frances talks about where she is from, and one of Nick's friends remarks, 'I didn't think Nick had culchie friends' (CWF, p. 56). Although the comment can be interpreted as disrespectful toward Frances' background, it also highlights how frivolous his friends regard Nick to be, by arguing that his choice of friends is based solely on their coming from an urban background. This is an example of men asserting their dominance in a male group by belittling the sexual exploits of other men or their inability to control their desire. Perhaps the fact that they are not named, nor are there any details about who they are, suggests that Nick is the most successful man in the group. As such, belittling him in such a way seems to be an attempt to figuratively move him down the male dominance order. Nick does not react to this or any of the previous comments, possibly suggesting that this kind of exchange is to be expected, that this is how male friends talk to each other.

Flood's (2008, pp. 349–353) exploration of the relationship between heterosexual male homosociality and men's sexual relations with women, as well as Prick *et al.*'s (2001) examination of male homosociality in classical American stag films, highlight an alleged primacy of homosociality over other kinship forms whereby men assert that their male friends come first and above all other people in their lives. However, Rooney presents a different kind of homosocial organisation. In the scene described earlier, Nick's male friends do not appear to be complementary of him, nor do they seem to want to publicly support or praise him in any way. Contrary to this, the exchange is clearly an attempt to belittle him by objectifying Frances in front of him and by reducing his potential for emotional connection to superficial attraction, heightened by the fact that he is married. This could be explained in light of Bird's (1996) argument regarding the role of competition as a necessary 'stage for establishing self both as an individual and as appropriately masculine' (p. 127). However, it is somewhat striking that Nick does not seem to be partaking in this. Rather, he ignores everyone else's comments, allowing Frances to defend herself and respond to Nick's friends while enjoying her doing so. 'It felt good to belittle Nick's friends, although they seemed harmless. Nick laughed, as if to himself at something he had just remembered' (CWF, p. 57). The dynamics in this scene are very interesting. In the first instance, it appears as if Nick's friends behave in such a manner so as to assert their dominance and sustain a sort of hierarchy of masculinity where they sit on top. Hammarén and Johansson (2014) explain how '[w]omen become a kind of currency men use to improve their ranking on the masculine social scale' (p. 2). However, not only does Nick remain disinterested in any sort of competition or even assertion of his masculine standing but he also is – at least regarding his socioeconomic standing and popularity – the most successful among his friends. Conditions that would challenge his identification with what is traditionally considered strong and successful masculinity, such as his mental health problems and his hospitalisation, are only presented later in the novel, and whether these friends of his are aware of these conditions is not clear. By the time this scene unfolds in the novel, Nick is presented as the successful one of his friends, while the others appear to be almost insignificant. The person who mocks Frances, for example, is 'one of the men' (CWF, p. 56), and that is as much as we learn about him. It can be argued that Nick is the only man of interest for the narrative at this point because he is Frances' interest, but it can be equally argued that Nick's social standing, regarding his social class as well as his fame, has afforded him a level of confidence that surpasses the unwritten rules of homosociality, thus contributing a novel dimension in the conceptualisation of homosociality. It should be noted that this confidence does not have to be across all aspects of one's life. As it is illustrated by Nick's character, the areas of his life that might be affording him such a level of confidence are limited to his social class and his popularity. In his private matters, he comes across as quite insecure, though this is a domain that he does not share with his friends.

Similar to the way Nick's friends talk about Frances the first time they see her at Melissa's party are Derek's comments about Louisa, a girl Nick accidentally dated once. This conversation takes place in France, while Melissa, Nick, and a group of their friends are staying at Valerie's villa in Étables. Derek is initially making fun of Nick for having gone through a period in his life where he did a lot of air travelling. Responding to Bobbi's comment about airports, 'Derek said: ah, Nick's old haunt' (CWF, p. 99). This sparks a discussion about Nick being 'a jetsetter' (CWF, p. 99), which very quickly moves toward a story about Nick having taken a girl who was working at the airport on a date. 'He's even had a wild affair with a stewardess, Derek said' (CWF, p. 99), though he stands corrected by Melissa who explains that the girl was working at the airport Starbucks café. It transpires that this was nothing near a 'wild affair' (CWF, p. 99) as Derek said. Rather, as a result of flying a lot, Nick had started talking to the girl working at the airport Starbucks café, and she asked him out for coffee in town. Nick agreed without thinking that this was a romantic date, which Derek doubted. 'You must have known at some level, said Derek. What she was after' (CWF, p. 100). In saying so, Derek arguably rejects the possibility of a friendship between a man and a woman, in line with empirical research which supports the same (Flood, 2008, p. 344), but he further questions Nick's ability to understand what a woman might want from him, insinuating that neither would a woman want to just be friendly with him, nor would it be possible for him not to know this. Further, Derek presents Nick as having been objectified by that woman who played the role expected of a man.

Similar exchanges are observed in *Beautiful World, Where Are You*, for example, when Felix is in Rome with Alice. One morning, when Alice is occupied with publicity events for her book, Felix strolls around Rome and chats with his male friends on WhatsApp. After posting a picture of the dome of St. Peter's Basilica to the group chat, his friends are asking him where he is and why he is not at work. Felix responds, 'Roma baby. Lmao. Here with some girl I met on tinder, ill tell you when im back', only to receive a response from one of his friends, Dave, reading, 'Wait what!! did a wealthy old lady pick you up on the internet?' (BWWAY, p. 85). Not only are certain notions of femininity embedded in Dave's response with stereotypes around older rich women having to pay younger men to accompany them but there is a sarcastic undertone with reference to Felix and his ability to form a genuine connection with a woman who can take him on a trip abroad. These interactions are not different to the ones discussed earlier between Nick and his friends. Similar discussions illustrating ideas around class and masculinity, as well as around female degradation as an affirmation of one's masculinity and a point of connection with other men, can be found in *Normal People* as well. These are further discussed in the next chapter, with attention to the notion of socialisation into maleness through homosocial encounters.

In addition to men belittling or undermining each other publicly, another important feature of homosocial organisation is their attitude toward emotional displays. Men appear to be actively trying to come across as indifferent even to things that they might be interested in, as is the case of Philip; they also become objects of criticism when they express a more emotional, sensitive, or caring response either toward others or toward themselves. An interesting aspect of Nick's limited interactions with other men is his attempt to maintain some distance from them by appearing to be imperturbable. An example of this can be found in the scene where Frances and Melissa have a conversation with a novelist after the launch of a new poetry anthology. Bobbi and Nick are getting drinks, and when they come back, the novelist starts talking to Nick. The narrator does not focus on the content of the conversation between the novelist and Nick; rather, they focus on the way Nick addresses the novelist. 'The novelist said something to Nick, and Nick replied with the word 'man', like: oh, sorry about that, man' (CWF, p. 45, emphasis in original). What is particularly interesting about this remark is that in the same chapter it becomes known that Nick has studied English and French at Trinity. No reasons have been presented as to consider him dismissive toward matters relevant to literature or art. Therefore, the level of informality, if not indifference, with which he addresses the novelist, whom he had not known prior to this event, could suggest an attempt to mask his engagement with topics such as literature and the arts; almost as if the use of a more colloquial register distances Nick from any public admission of him having a side that cares about literature and could therefore be perceived to be sensitive. This appears to be in contrast with the private conversations he has with Frances, including conversations about literature, which are generally more in-depth and engaged and could explain why Frances is surprised by his demeanour on this occasion.

The repudiation of interests, activities, or even sentiments that are stereotypically associated with the feminine is very well documented in the literature of homosociality (e.g. Bird, 1996, pp. 125–127; Oransky and Marecek, 2009, pp. 227–231). Findings from empirical research support the idea that men are actively avoiding public manifestations of anything that resembles the feminine in an attempt to maintain their hierarchically dominant position not only in relation to the feminine but, most importantly, in relation to other men. Reporting on the findings of her study, Bird (1996, p. 126) explains that the men who took part declared that acceding to stereotypically feminine activities, or even interests, publicly would warrant their marginalisation and, ultimately, exclusion from their homosocial network. In this instance, and in light of what has been discussed so far in this chapter, Nick does not appear particularly invested in creating, let alone maintaining, homosocial networks with other men. If anything, his behaviour toward other men signifies an apathy for male kinship. Bird (1996) reminds us, though, that 'although individual conceptualisations of masculinity depart from the hegemonic norm, nonhegemonic meanings are suppressed due to perceptions of "appropriate" masculinity' (p. 127, emphasis in original). In other words, Nick's own conceptualisation of masculinity, his gender identity, might be different to mainstream hegemonic understandings of the masculine identity. However, this does not prohibit him from performing his masculinity, his gender role, in a conventional hegemonic manner.

In Rooney's novels, men appear to have to diminish their affective experiences as well as to have to downplay their own or each other's physical health-related problems. For example, upon arriving in Étables to spend some time with Nick, Melissa, and their friends, Frances and Bobbi notice immediately that Nick looks unwell. 'Were you always this skinny? Bobbi said. I remember you bigger' (CWF, p. 98). It appears evident from the way he looks that his health is deteriorated. However, Derek, Nick's friend, lessens the severity of Nick's illness. 'He's been sick, said Derek. He had bronchitis, he's very sensitive about it. It was pneumonia, Nick said' (CWF, p. 98). Further downplaying the importance of the illness, Derek also makes a sarcastic comment about the way Nick has dealt with it. Sensitive is an adjective that men commonly associate with the feminine (Oransky and Marecek, 2009, p. 235); that is, Derek is almost saying that Nick 'is being a girl about it'. In doing so, we understand that there are certain expectations regarding not only how men are allowed to experience an illness but also how they are supposed to express their experience to fellow men. This is supported by medical literature (Galdas, Cheater and Marshall, 2005) that highlights 'traditional masculinity' (p. 621) as a leading cause in men's inability to seek help when they are physically ill. Actually, research findings support that men are less inclined to ask for help when they are unwell and that they are not supposed to do so. They are also expected to trivialise their conditions, physical or otherwise (e.g. Möller-Leimkühler, 2002, pp. 2–4; Addis and Mahalik, 2003, pp. 7–8). Indeed, Nick does not even address his illness, let alone ask for help; rather, he seems to be isolating himself from others, without explaining what he is going through.

Similar expectations regarding masculinity as non-femininity are observed not only in the domain of pain or illness control but also in notions and perceptions around beauty. While in France, and on a day the group is on the beach, Derek makes a remark that highlights commonly held notions around masculinity and beauty whereby one's interest in their physical appearance can be interpreted as a sign of them being less of a man. 'Nick liked to go swimming and then come back out of the water glistening wet and looking like an advertisement for cologne. Derek said he found it emasculating. . . . Derek said: Melissa, does he spend a lot of time preening?' (CWF, pp. 117–118). From this exchange, we can assume that it is not the fact that Nick has a beautiful body that triggers Derek; rather, that he is so handsome that is intimidating for other men. And yet, instead of genuine interest in the ways in which Nick maintains his physical appearance, Derek resorts to demeaning comments, challenging Nick's masculinity and accusing him of being self-indulgent regarding his own looks. Indeed, Derek's *idée fixe* about what masculinity is and how it should be manifested can be observed in a later scene where the group is playing a game in the evening, and because they keep the lights on and the windows open, 'a moth would fly in through the window and Nick would catch it in his hands and throw it back out again, while Derek encouraged him to kill it' (CWF, p. 127). Not only do we observe a more aggressive form of masculinity being exhibited by Derek but we can further observe that the exchange between the two men, with Derek telling Nick how to act, suggests that any sign of sensitivity is to be eradicated. Bird (1996, p. 128) accounts for such behaviours, suggesting that competition is an important characteristic of male homosocial bonds which, even when the men involved are not inherently competitive as individuals, always manifests itself in male-to-male forms of kinship. With this in mind, both instances described earlier – that is, Derek's disparaging of Nick for being very handsome and for not being abusive toward an insect – can be understood as instances of competition where Derek publicly asserts his dominance over Nick.

Paying close attention to the instances where Nick engages with other men, and those instances when he avoids doing so, in *Conversations with Friends*, as well as similar instances that can be found in the other novels by Rooney, encourages consideration of a particular type of homosociality that has not been identified in scholarly literature on the subject, that of the impossible homosociality. By this, I refer to the limited and apparently meaningless bonds men create with other men as a result of a rigid adherence to normative notions about expected expressions of masculinity. Indeed, I use the term meaningless here to refer to the limited and not substantial interactions men have with one another. However, as the discussion has shown, these interactions are meaningful in their meaninglessness in that they provide ample evidence of how homosociality is organised and structured in ways that render it impossible. The chapter provides ample examples where Nick actively avoids connecting with other men, or, when he does, he stands in as an opportunity for the other men to affirm their dominant position in an assumed hierarchy of masculinity by letting them discredit him. The chapter refers briefly to similar instances that are observable in *Normal People* and *Beautiful World, Where Are You*. These novels are more extensively focused on in subsequent chapters of this book to illustrate other features of homosociality which point toward novel expressions of masculinity and male-to-male homosocial behaviours.

References

Addis, M. E. and Mahalik, J. R. (2003) 'Men, masculinity, and the contexts of help seeking', *American Psychologist*, 58, pp. 5–14. https://doi.org/10.1037/0003-066X.58.1.5.

Anderson, E. (2008) 'Inclusive masculinity in a fraternal setting', *Men and Masculinities*, 10, pp. 604–620. https://doi.org/10.1177/1097184X06291907.

Anderson, E. (2009) *Inclusive masculinities: The changing nature of masculinity*. London: Routledge.

Badin, A. (2016) 'Between men: Homosocial desire and the dynamics of masculinity in the novels of Rachid O. and Abdellah Taïa', *Contemporary French and Francophone Studies*, 20(1), pp. 111–120. https://doi.org/10.1080/17409292.2016.1120558.

Bell, R. R. (1981) 'Friendships of women and of men', *Psychology of Women Quarterly*, 5(3), pp. 402–417. https://doi.org/10.1111/j.1471-6402.1981.tb00582.x.

Bird, S. R. (1996) 'Welcome to the men's club: Homosociality and the maintenance of hegemonic masculinity', *Gender & Society*, 10(2), pp. 120–132. https://doi.org/10.1177/089124396010002002.

Caldwell, M. A. and Peplau, L. A. (1982) 'Sex differences in same-sex friendship', *Sex Roles: A Journal of Research*, 8, pp. 721–732. https://doi.org/10.1007/BF00287568.

Fischer, J. L. and Narus, L. R. (1981) 'Sex roles and intimacy in same sex and other sex relationships', *Psychology of Women Quarterly*, 5(3), pp. 444–455. https://doi.org/10.1111/j.1471-6402.1981.tb00585.x.

Flood, M. (2008) 'Men, sex, and homosociality: How bonds between men shape their sexual relations with women', *Men and Masculinities*, 10(3), pp. 339–359. https://doi.org/10.1177/1097184X06287761.

Galdas, P. M., Cheater, F. and Marshall, P. (2005) 'Men and health help-seeking behaviour: Literature review', *Journal of Advanced Nursing*, 49(6), pp. 616–623. https://doi.org/10.1111/j.1365-2648.2004.03331.x.

Gilmartin, S. K. (2007) 'Crafting heterosexual masculine identities on campus: College men talk about romantic love', *Men and Masculinities*, 9(4), pp. 530–539. https://doi.org/10.1177/1097184X05284994.

Hammarén, N. and Johansson, T. (2014) 'Homosociality: In between power and intimacy', *Sage Open*, 4(1), pp. 1–11. https://doi.org/10.1177/2158244013518057.

Ibson, J. (2002) *Picturing men: A century of male relationships in everyday American photography*. Chicago: University of Chicago Press.

Möller-Leimkühler, A. M. (2002) 'Barriers to help-seeking by men: A review of sociocultural and clinical literature with particular reference to depression', *Journal of Affective Disorders*, 71(1–3), pp. 1–9. https://doi.org/10.1016/s0165-0327(01)00379-2.

Oransky, M. and Marecek, J. (2009) '"I'm not going to be a girl": Masculinity and emotions in boys' friendships and peer groups', *Journal of Adolescent Research*, 24(2), pp. 218–241. https://doi.org/10.1177/0743558408329951.

Prick, A., Cunt, I., Hard, R. U. and Waugh, T. (2001) 'Homosociality in the classical American stag film: Off-screen, on-screen', *Sexualities*, 4(3), pp. 275–291. https://doi.org/10.1177/136346001004003001.

Rachid, O. (1996) *Plusiers Vies*. Paris: Gallimard.

Rooney, S. (2017) *Conversations with friends*. London: Faber & Faber.

Rooney, S. (2018) *Normal people*. London: Faber & Faber.

Rooney, S. (2021) *Beautiful world, where are you*. London: Faber & Faber.

Rose, S. M. (1985) 'Same- and cross-sex friendships and the psychology of homosociality', *Sex Roles*, 12(1), pp. 63–74. https://doi.org/10.1007/BF00288037.

Underwood, M. (2018) '"We're all gonna make It brah": Homosocial relations, vulnerability and intimacy in an online bodybuilding community', in A. S. Dobson, B. Robards and N. Carah (eds.) *Digital intimate publics and social media*. Basingstoke: Palgrave Macmillan, pp. 161–176. https://doi.org/10.1007/978-3-319-97607-5_10.

2 Male Homosociality in the (Un)Making

By focusing primarily on *Conversations with Friends*, the previous chapter highlights superficial relationships men often engage with. In doing so, the concept of impossible male homosociality is introduced as a way to illustrate men's adherence to societal gender scripts, which, in turn, results in men finding themselves isolated from one another, unable to form meaningful bonds. Building on this, this chapter focuses primarily on *Normal People* and, in particular, on Connell's relationships with other teenage boys during their time in high school. The chapter examines how male homosociality is negotiated and defined in childhood, suggesting that men are primed to refrain from establishing close relationships with one another in fear of 'compromising' their masculinity in public or, perhaps more accurately, the public's expectations of their masculinity. With the exception of sports contexts, which appear to provide opportunities for approved emotional and physical closeness, teenage boys seem to engage in limited interactions with one another. These often centre around boasting about their fathers' achievements and their sexual prowess and objectifying girls and women. By analysing such instances of male-to-male interactions, the chapter illustrates the relationship among hegemony, masculinities, and homosociality and examines how this relationship is structured during men's formative years. The exception of sports-related contexts which provide men and teenage boys with a safe space to engage in public displays of intimacy with one another is significant in that it highlights how important intimacy is for men even if they do not acknowledge it to be so.

Normal People provides an opportunity for readers to observe how teenage boys negotiate rules of homosocial behaviour and, in turn, examine the foundations of male homosociality that come to affect not only men's relationships with one another but also men's behaviour in general. Readers observe Connell interacting with his male peers for the first time in the novel during a soccer match right after he scores the winning goal. This event is significant not only for highlighting Connell's athletic abilities but also for encouraging the suspension of any socially imposed limitations over the way he, his classmates, and his teachers are to behave with, and in the presence of, each other. Anderson

DOI: 10.4324/9781032644974-3

(2014) explains that athletic environments provide men with spaces where they can come into emotional and physical contact with one another in ways that they cannot do in different contexts as a result of overt policing of gendered behaviour which, as McCormack (2012) demonstrates, is a result of societal homophobia.

> Everyone screamed, even Marianne, and Karen threw her arm around Marianne's waist and squeezed it. They were cheering together, they had seen something magical which dissolved the ordinary social relations between them. Miss Keaney was whistling and stamping her feet.
>
> (NP, p. 12)

Within this atmosphere of togetherness and unity, Connell's excitement results in him somatising his emotions. 'On the pitch Connell and Aidan embraced like reunited brothers' (NP, p. 12). Aidan is Connell's classmate and teammate who contributes to Connell's scoring the goal by crossing the ball to him. However, prior to this moment, the two young men are not seen to have any physical interaction with one another, nor to engage in any kind of communication. The particular incident can come across as insignificant regarding the relation between two teenage boys and the way in which they express this relation publicly. However, another incident that appears much later in the novel contributes to the significance of this public embrace between Connell and Aidan. Three years later, Connell attends the funeral of another one of his classmates, Rob. Through an analepsis, the narrator describes a very similar event that occurred when Connell was in fifth year. The narrator explains that at that time, during a soccer match, Connell also scores a goal, not the winning one that time, and

> Rob had leapt onto the pitch to embrace him. He screamed Connell's name, and began to kiss his head with wild exuberant kisses. It was only one-all, and there were still twenty minutes left on the clock. But that was their world then. Their feelings were suppressed so carefully in everyday life, forced into smaller and smaller spaces, until seemingly minor events took on insane and frightening significance. It was permissible to touch each other and cry during football matches.
>
> (NP, p. 212)

The narrator highlights the significance of the embrace not only as a physical expression of strong emotions such as happiness and/or admiration but also as the symbolic transgression of societal rules that regulate how men are to negotiate their feelings at an individual level as well as how they are to engage with other men. Indeed, in the context of sports, physical touch is not seen as a transgression, but, as it is further analysed later, this can be viewed as a form of escapism from the constant policing of masculine behaviour. That is, the emphasis that is placed on these instances of physical embrace during sports events in the narrative might illustrate a compensation mechanism deployed by teenage boys who use sports as an excuse to come into physical – and emotional – contact with their male friends without being reprimanded for doing so. It is important to note here that sports is not suggested to be the sole context in which boys and men can be vulnerable with each other. Rather, it is argued that in this context, boys and men can express their vulnerability without the fear of being judged for transgressing boundaries of appropriate gendered behaviour.

As the study by Oransky and Marecek (2009, p. 225) suggests, boys are socialised into maleness by suppressing expressions of emotions and by avoiding participating in communal emotional experiences with other boys at all costs, except when participating in sports. The degree of this suppression is further highlighted by the narrator who explains that 'Connell still remembers the too-hard grip of his [Rob's] arms' (NP, p. 212). That is, more than a decade later, Connell finds himself contemplating the embrace and the effect this has had not only on himself but also on his friend Rob. This is immediately contrasted with another analepsis which presents Rob in a different light when he is 'showing [his classmates] those photographs of Lisa's naked body' while they were at the Debs (NP, p. 212). The quick transition from emotional to indifferent and possibly loutish behaviour signifies Rob's rite of passage into manhood. The narrator continues, 'Nothing had meant more to Rob than the approval of others; to be thought well of, to be a person of status. He would have betrayed any confidence, any kindness, for the promise of social acceptance' (NP, p. 212). And yet, striving for social acceptance and the suggestion that the affective side of Rob's threatens his opportunities to be acknowledged, accepted, and respected are not presented here as his individual characteristics. 'He [Connell] had been the same way himself, or worse. He had just wanted to be normal, to conceal the parts of himself that he found shameful and confusing' (NP, p. 212). By not differentiating between Rob and Connell's experiences, the narrative points toward a universality in the way young boys are made to understand the world in a manner where emotions are not normal, while parts of themselves, such as their need to embrace each other, to physically touch their friends and share their emotions, are to be concealed as shameful and confusing except on the soccer pitch. Indeed, recent empirical evidence confirms the significance of educational settings as the primary context for the formation of homosocial relations (Thomas, 2019, p. 832). What is of particular importance is that at this stage, the foundations for future homosocial relations are built. Based on the male homosocial relations that emerge in *Normal People*, it appears that teenage boys need to engage in closer relations with one another, physical or otherwise, but tend to do so in the context of athleticism and sports.

Indeed, sports can provide men and teenage boys an opportunity to base their relation on the possibility of accomplishing a goal. In that sense, within the context of sports, societal rules of masculine and, by extension, homosocial behaviour are halted because what drives men's relations is not an emotional motive but a rather pragmatic one: the accomplishment of a material goal.

Empirical studies endorse the significance of the mutual investment toward the achievement of a goal, typical in sport settings, as an enabling factor toward the creation of male homosocial relations (Vigil, 2007, p. 144) as well as its contribution toward their material foundation (Curry, 2000). As such, any kind of physical proximity and, to a certain extent, an emotional one is to be understood as an important facilitator toward more effective cooperation which, in turn, can lead to the achievement of the shared goal in focus (Benenson, 2013, p. 6). Ibson's (2002) study confirms that physical proximity among – and its significance for – heterosexual men is historically contingent. McCormack and Anderson (2014, pp. 110–111) demonstrate that the possibility of being perceived to be gay is reported as the primary reason for the physical distancing among heterosexual boys and men. However, an increase in the articulation of the significance of physical closeness in building friendships with other boys and men has been observed recently (Hruschka, 2010, p. 121; McCormack, 2012). This suggests that sports can function as an excuse of sorts for teenage boys and men to freely connect with one another at a physical level without the possibility of being labelled gay and, in turn, be marginalised or discriminated against. This explains why, as the narrator in *Normal People* explains, closeness is normalised in sports, which then allows Connell, Aidan, and Rob to express their affection for one another physically and verbally only within the context of sports. However, such expressive – and performative – affection is to be dropped when outside the sports arena and be replaced by behaviour that affirms their (heterosexual) masculinity (Anderson, 2014). This is perhaps why immediately after reading about Rob's outburst of admiration and affection toward Connell follows the scene of him circulating a girl's naked pictures among his friends that was discussed earlier – an act that publicly confirms his heterosexuality as well as his detachment from any sort of affective side that could jeopardise the way his peers perceive him and, in turn, their acceptance of him. Sports, both in life and in the novel, becomes a refuge where teenage boys, and men, can stop policing their behaviour toward other men. Outside of this, though, it is almost imperative that they engage in as much limited and meaningless interactions as possible.

The only topic that Connell and his friends appear to be sincere about and interested in engaging at a more meaningful level is family and, in particular, their fathers. 'On nights out his friends sometimes raise the subject of his [Connell's] father, like it's something deep and meaningful they can only talk about when they're drunk. Connell finds this depressing' (NP, p. 46). The narrator is vague as to whether 'this' refers to the alcohol or the absence of his father, and highlights the need for these young boys to be drunk before they are able to discuss a topic that might be sensitive or just important to them. Possibly this would allow them not only to process situations that might be challenging for them, such as a difficult relationship with their father, but it would also allow them to talk about this in front of other male friends, turning affective discussions into slips of the tongue caused by alcohol consumption. It would appear alien for a teenage boy to share his thoughts about his father in front of male peers in this novel. As the discussion that follows in this chapter suggests, they would ask this person not to be 'so gay', meaning not to show emotional vulnerability (Morin and Garfinkle, 1978, p. 39). Connell appears surprised by the importance his peers give to their fathers and the relationship they have with them. Since he has never met his father, he has no relationship with him. Further to this, though, he seems to have distanced himself from the significance this figure could have had in his life. 'He never thinks about the man who got Lorraine pregnant, why would he?' (NP, p. 46). This detachment could explain the overall detachment he exhibits when it comes to his relationships with his male peers. However, they also seem to be having similar issues with connecting at a deeper level with each other despite the fact that they have some kind of relationship with their fathers. That is, even though they have their fathers in their lives, they are equally unable, or willing to, connect with their male peers at a more meaningful level.

> His friends seem so obsessed with their own fathers, obsessed with emulating them or being different from them in specific ways. Whey they fight with their fathers, the fights always seem to mean one thing on the surface but conceal another secret meaning beneath.
>
> (NP, p. 46)

The relationship between Connell's male peers and their fathers is another instance of male homosociality that is observed in the novel. However, it appears that this relationship is a non-reciprocal one. The father figure appears as a point of reference that determines the behaviour of the teenage boys in relation to them: either imitating or differentiating themselves from their fathers. However, for Connell this is different. His homosociality is likely to have been impacted by the absence of his father in that he does not have the means to navigate his relationships with his male peers. Despite this, though, the topic of the father, present or absent, and the relationships the young boys have with them presents one of very few opportunities these teenage boys have to engage in more meaningful interactions with one other.

Except for discussing their relationships with their fathers, all other interactions among male peers at school in *Normal People* are almost exclusively superficial or focused on their sexual experiences with girls. When Marianne asks Connell whether his friends are aware of his love for books, for example, he explains that their interests would not be very similar to his. 'They wouldn't be interested in that stuff. . . . They have their own interests. I don't think they'd be reading books about racism and all that' (NP, p. 14). In the discussion that follows between the two, Marianne appears to be judgemental about the behaviour of some of Connell's peers. '[T]hey're too busy bragging about who they're having sex with, she said' (NP, p.14). Connell is aware that his friends' comments about women sometimes cross a line, but he seems to be accepting them for who they are. 'They do some stuff that goes a bit over the line and that would annoy me obviously. But at the end of the day they're my friends', he says (NP, p. 15). It is very interesting that Connell is aware of his friends' behaviour but seems to be accepting it as 'normal'. He himself has been their target, but he makes no effort to change this. For example, the narrator tells us that Connell, before having sex with Marianne, would only have sex with

> girls who went on to tell the whole school about it afterwards. He'd had to hear his actions repeated back to him later in the locker room: his errors, and, so much worse, his excruciating attempts at tenderness, performed in gigantic pantomime.
>
> (NP, p. 21)

Despite being teased, if not ridiculed, by his peers in the locker rooms, Connell never appears annoyed or hurt, not initially at least; not even when his friends talk about his mother's physical appearance, though not in a sexual manner, just praising her for being beautiful (NP, p. 46). When he is with his friends, Connell seems to enjoy their company. One day, for example, Marianne observes him smiling while having lunch with his friends and seemingly having a good time with them (NP, p. 17). For some scholars, the type of 'locker room' talk that Connell's friends appear to be employing, especially with regards to each other's sexual experiences, is an integral part of teenage boys' socialisation into becoming men. For example, Holland *et al.* (2004, p. 78) describe this as 'central to the way that young men learn about masculinity'. Further, existing scholarship on teenage boys' relations suggests that Connell's behaviour is not surprising. That is, even when teenage boys do not necessarily adopt hostile behaviours toward girls or one another, they are still likely to participate in, or at least not challenge, such conversations (Bridges and Pascoe, 2014, p. 251; Ging, 2017, p. 3). At this stage, it appears that Connell's inaction regarding his peers' hostilities reflects an overall understanding of such teenage behaviour as almost inevitable and inescapable. This is challenged later on in the novel with Connell providing a reason as to why he does not verbalise his disagreement with the way his friends talk and act. Scholars such as Haywood *et al.* (2017, pp. 59–62) call for a more nuanced approach to the study of homosociality, criticising descriptive and simplistic views that situate homosociality as a rite of passage into hegemonic masculinity. Connell's reflection on what contributes to his inactivity in this incident illustrates such nuanced understanding of male homosociality which will be discussed in detail later in the chapter. To do this, though, it is important for the discussion to turn first to the way sex, and the sexualisation of women and teenage girls, is used by Connell's peers.

In addition to using sex, and their sexual 'achievements', as a way to bond, teenage boys in Rooney's work use teenage girls as a way to connect with each other, though in an objectified and sexualised manner. The narrator in *Normal People*, for example, explains that boys often denigrate girls as liars when they talk to one another: 'He [Connell]'d heard from guys in school that sometimes girls made up stories about themselves for attention, saying bad things had happened to them and stuff like that' (NP, p. 52). What is interesting is not only what boys say about girls and how this can affect the ways in which they can form and navigate their relationships with them in the future. This is problematic in its own right. However, it is also interesting that such discussions comprise the arguably limited interactions boys have with one another. As such, they are not only guarded against tapping into and sharing their own emotional world with each other, but they are also meant to discard emotions as a sly way one can get attention. This is further illustrated by the fact that most, if not all, discussions teenage boys tend to have about girls are discussions about sex. After the fundraiser event, for instance,

> Eric slung an arm around his [Connell's] shoulder and said: Go on, tell us. Did you get the ride the other night? I heard you looked very cosy heading off together, said Rob. Did anything happen? Eric said. Be honest. . . . I bet he did get a cheeky ride, said Rob. He'd never tell us anyway.
>
> (NP, p. 53)

The boys enquire whether Connell and Marianne had sex after leaving the fundraising event together. However, in their exchanges, there is no room for any discussion about feelings Connell might be having toward Marianne. 'I wouldn't hold it against you, Eric said, she's not a bad-looking girl when she makes an effort' (NP, p. 53). Toward the end of this scene, Connell becomes physically sick when reflecting on how he has been treating Marianne as a result of conforming to an assumed norm that does not allow boys to have genuine feelings for girls (NP. p. 54). However, the scene provides evidence of how male bonds are created based on ideas around expected masculine behaviour. At a later instance in the novel, after Rob's funeral, Connell recalls the last message he received from his now-dead friend which reads, 'are u riding her [Marianne]?? NICE haha' (NP, p. 205). Although the discourse of the objectification of the female and her reduction to a sexual trophy remains the same, the more positive sort of response that Rob communicates in this message can possibly attest to a suppressed need to actually lift each other up. In no synchronous conversation among male peers do we see a positive reinforcement being stated. However, Rob seems to be more comfortable saying something positive to his friend in a text, a sign of approval of sorts which is kept in private between the two of them.

Later in the novel, Marianne reveals that she was bullied by Eric and Rob in front of everyone at her school. This illustrates how the objectification and denigration of women stands as an opportunity for teenage boys to interact with each other, as if the act of belittling and hurting a teenage girl is an excuse for boys to find some common ground with each other. 'It's true they did bully her. Eric called her 'flat-chested' once, in front of everyone, and Rob, laughing, scrambled to whisper something in Eric's ear, some affirmation, or some further insult too vulgar to speak out loud' (NP, pp. 225–226, emphasis in original). In this incident, Rob takes notice of Eric's behaviour, and, instead of challenging it, he seems to be reinforcing it. The narrator explains that Rob 'was also a very insecure person, obsessed with popularity, and his desperation had made him cruel' (NP, p. 226). In this instance, bullying behaviour is discussed as a symptom of problematic relations primarily among teenage boys. It appears that to be seen by his male peers, Rob resorts to hurting Marianne, imitating Eric's behaviour in public. In doing so, Rob offers his public support to Eric, Eric acknowledges Rob's move, and the two can maintain a friendship on the grounds of a shared hostility toward girls, instead of a shared love for one another. Hostility masks love, because love is not allowed between boys. This incident suggests that teenage boys are not unaware of hostile behaviour. As illustrated in this scene, Rob follows Eric's lead and responds by approving this behaviour and further contributing to it. A very similar behaviour is observed by Eric who mirrors this aggressive behaviour at the Debs fundraiser event where he belittles Marianne. More specifically, when 'someone's brothers or cousins maybe, or just men in their twenties who like to hang around school fundraisers' (NP, p. 39) appear at the event, one of them makes a move on Marianne. She expresses her discomfort, but her male classmates ignore her and treat her distress as a joke. However, what is interesting is that they only respond to the situation following the cue of the older man suggesting that their response does not represent their authentic understanding of the situation; rather, they respond in a manner that will make them accepted by the older male peer in attendance.

> Let me get you a drink, the man says. What are you having? No, thanks, says Marianne. The man slips an arm around her shoulders then. . . . She tries to shrug him off but he doesn't let go. One of his friends starts laughing, and Eric laughs along.
>
> (NP, p. 39)

Although not clear at this stage in the narration, Eric does not react to the situation unprompted. He first reads his peers' reactions and then follows along. Arguably, Eric does not find the situation funny; he might even understand the severity of what is happening to Marianne. However, he does not challenge his friend's behaviour; he encourages it. A few moments later, this is confirmed when, after Marianne leaves in shock because Eric's friend touched her breasts, Eric adopts a more apologetic stance. 'Here, look, it was just a bit of fun, says Eric. Pat's [the friend who molested Marianne] actually a sound enough guy if you get to know him' (NP, p. 40). Pat is not present during this exchange, suggesting that Eric understands that what Pat did was not right but is afraid of confronting him so as not to risk losing his respect by coming across as sensitive. A few moments later, Connell explains to Marianne that '[t]hey just think Pat is great because he has these parties in his house sometimes. Apparently if you have house parties it's okay to mess with people' (NP, p. 42). What becomes apparent through these interactions is that hostile behaviours that men – or teenage boys in this instance – adopt, and witness, toward women and girls do not result from a personal need to inflict psychological pain on to them; rather, they appear to be performative markers of adherence to homosocial codes of behaviour. That is, hostility toward females functions as a signifier of males' interest – if not need – to engage in homosocial relations.

The behaviours discussed so far are consistent with recent empirical evidence of teenage boys' behaviour and the role of female objectification in the maintenance of homosociality. In particular, a study by Bolton *et al.* (2022) contextualises female abuse within the context of homosociality in Ireland. Bolton's team interviewed 28 young people, focusing on how they understand violence against women and how this functions in relation to their relationships with their peers. One of their findings suggests that '[v]erbal harassment, objectification and violence were identified by participants not as the simple practice of *individual* men enacting individually held problematic attitudes and hostile beliefs about women, but a collectively based practice *among* men' (p. 9, emphasis in original). In essence, the way Connell's friends talk about their female peers, and women in general, is significant, not only in that it reveals overall hostile and degrading societal attitudes toward women; rather, it is significant because it has a homosocial function: it enables teenage men to create a bond with one another. That is not to say that this is a practice that should be promoted for the benefits of establishing and maintaining male friendship. Quite the contrary: this suggests that young men desire and need close friendships with one another but rely on despicable behaviours that victimise women to create intimacy. The novel urges for a reflection over the lack of resources teenage boys have, beyond sports and goal-oriented activities which were discussed earlier, that would allow them to form stronger bonds with one another. Rob's text message further attests to this. Even though his language remains derogatory, his tone is arguably not so. When in the company of other men, Rob exhibits a hostile behaviour that is to be read and approved by other men; however, in the more intimate interaction that the text message provides, he shows a more genuine interest in Connell whereby asking about Connell's sexual encounters can be interpreted as a pretext for 'having a good time', or 'being happy'. This is not a surprising contrast. Scholars have long argued about the performative element of masculinity which is to be caught and validated by the gaze of other men (Schwalbe, 2014). Additionally, though, recent research points toward a change in the way men, and young boys, negotiate their friendly relationships with other men, suggesting an increasing awareness of the importance of emotional connection, one which is based on positive reinforcement and vulnerability often found in the bromance relationship (Robinson, Anderson and White, 2018, pp. 99–100). Although the text message Rob sends to Connell does not illustrate a bromance, it does provide an indication of Rob's desire for a more intimate connection with Connell, one that is not influenced by societal pressures over masculine behaviour. This is only one instance, though, which is not observed in the relationships the young male characters have with one another. The remaining part of the novel about the teenage years of Connell and Marianne's lives confirms what is discussed in the previous chapter: a repudiation of any sort of emotion in male-to-male homosocial relations.

Even within the context of sex, Connell refuses to talk to his male friends about Marianne. Instead, he chooses to keep their relationship a secret, even though he knows that this is hurting Marianne and himself.

> That's just the way it has to be. If people found out what he has been doing with Marianne, in secret, while ignoring her every day in school, his life would be over. He would walk down the hallway and people's eyes would follow him, like he was a serial killer or worse.
>
> (NP, p. 27)

At this moment, the narration is unclear as to what would trouble his peers more about him: the fact that he is able to live a double life, or that he might be having genuine feelings for another person who is not part of their social circle. Arguably, it is not his friends that he is afraid of; rather, it is the realisation of who he actually is that he avoids by keeping his affair with Marianne a secret.

> His friends don't think of him as a deviant person, a person who could say to Marianne Sheridan, in broad daylight, completely sober: Is it okay if I come in your mouth? With his friends he acts normal. He and Marianne have their own private life in his room where no one can bother them, so there's no reason to mix up the separate worlds
>
> (NP, p. 27)

It becomes progressively clear that Connell's reluctance to engage in more meaningful relationships with his male peers is because he is afraid to see that he is what he despises in them. He believes that sharing his sexual desires, a practice that is common among male peers, will make him deviant and cost the approval of others.

> He can have the respect of someone like Marianne and also be well liked in school, he can form secret opinions and preferences, no conflict has to arise, he never has to choose one thing over another. With only a little subterfuge he can live two entirely separate existences, never confronting the ultimate question of what to do with himself or what kind of person he is.
>
> (NP, p. 28)

Connell commits to keeping his relationship with Marianne a secret, believing that this will contribute to him being accepted by his peers. At school, Marianne is seen as an oddball, and an intimate relationship with her could make Connell an oddball by association. And yet, when later in the story he finds out that his peers knew all along about the fact that he was sexually involved with Marianne (NP, pp. 76–77), he continues concealing the affective aspect of their relationship, ensuring that his friends will not accuse him of having feelings for her, which, in turn, could mean that he is less of a man. 'Do you think we don't know you were riding her? he [Eric] said. And what's the story there? You were just doing it for the laugh or what?' to which Connell responds, 'You know me' (NP, p. 77), ensuring that his friend will not even assume that there could be anything more than a sexual relationship between Connell and Marianne, one in which Connell used Marianne just because he felt like it.

Building on the concept of compulsory heterosexuality (Rich, 1980), Pascoe (2011, p. 86, emphasis in original) offers 'compulsive heterosexuality' to explain the almost-obsessive dependence of teenage boys and men on public confirmation of their dominance within male homosocial contexts. Pascoe (2011, p. 86) discusses this in relation to female subjects. That is, she explains that for men, female and submissive become tautological entities, which, in turn, is what allows them to assert their dominance in the eyes, and judgement, of other men. Arguably, Connell's investment in keeping his relationship with Marianne a secret from his peers can be considered a way for him to maintain his dominant position over her, a form of psychological violence exerted over Marianne by telling her that their peers should not find out about them because then Connell's social standing will change. At the same time, though, Connell's inability to admit his emotions toward Marianne to his male friends can also be understood as a symptom of *compulsive heterosexuality*. In that sense, by talking about the feelings he has for Marianne, Connell risks losing his position in an assumed hierarchy of masculinities whereby those associated with qualities which are stereotypically attached to femininity are subordinated by those associated with qualities that are stereotypically attached to masculinity (Schippers, 2007, p. 95). Hierarchies and typologies of masculinities that identify subject positions of men and create power dynamics have been put forward by many scholars (e.g. Connell, 1995; Messner, 2004). What these models have in common is an understanding of the tensions that exist within and among different expressions of masculinity. Acknowledging his emotional attraction to Marianne would possibly place him in a subordinate position, one which is 'situationally constructed as lesser than or aberrant and deviant to hegemonic masculinity . . . as well as dominant/dominating masculinities' (Messerschmidt, 2018, p. 126). For a study on male homosociality, what is important through Connell's character and his relationships with his male peers is an understanding of homosociality as a locus of tensions over constructions and displays of masculinities. Further, what makes these tensions and, by extension, these types of masculinities hegemonic is the apparent consent provided by those who benefit and those who seemingly suffer from such stratification.

To illustrate this further, Connell might be seen as suffering from having to keep his emotions secret and from jeopardising his relationship with Marianne. Nonetheless, a very brief remark in the latter part of the novel helps illuminate how Connell understands the rules of homosociality at play while in secondary school; that is, how he needs to act in order for him not to challenge the hierarchically masculine order and lose the benefits he has from it, and he chooses to act accordingly. While at Rob's funeral, and upon observing Marianne responding to a sarcastic comment made by Eric, an old classmate of hers, the narrator says,

> Connell watched Marianne . . ., and he felt in awe of her naturalness, her easy way of moving through the world. It hadn't been like that in school, quite the opposite. Back then Connell had been the one who understood how to behave, while Marianne had just aggravated everyone.
>
> (NP, p. 212)

For Connell, secondary school is a time where simply being oneself – expressing one's feelings honestly and sharing affective responses in an authentic manner with one's peers – is enough to 'aggravate' everyone. Instead, concealing his emotions and refraining from expressing his disagreement with his peers were what he means by saying he 'understood how to behave' (NP, p. 212), suggesting that there is an unwritten code for appropriate behaviour by which teenagers have to abide. Indeed, in one of the very rare instances where Connell disagrees with the behaviour of his male friends, they respond to him in a demeaning manner. At the night of the Debs, one of the female students, Lisa, drinks a lot of alcohol and loses consciousness. Rob takes advantage of this and starts showing naked pictures of hers to his male friends.

> Eric laughed and tapped parts of Lisa's body on-screen with his fingers. Connell sat there looking at the phone and then said quietly: Bit fucked-up showing these to people, isn't it? With a loud sigh Rob locked the phone and put it back in his pocket. You've gotten awfully fucking gay about things lately, he said.
>
> (NP, p. 76)

Typical among secondary school male students (Short, 2013), Rob seems to be using 'gay' as misnomer for soft, emotional, sensitive, with the additional implication that such behaviour marks a difference between Connell and the rest of the boys which, if not checked, can lead to Connell being left out of the boy's group. This could reflect an underlying homophobic attitude (McGuffey and Rich, 1999, p. 116). However, as Pascoe (2011, pp. 52–83) demonstrates, the fag – in this instance gay – trope is enacted as a regulatory mechanism, a reminder of sorts, of the limits of heterosexual masculine behaviour. Thus, it functions as an acknowledgement by Connell's male peers of him deviating from an assumed male script that the rest of them adhere to.

In *Normal People*, there are two instances where Connell's detachment from his group of friends is highlighted. When Marianne stops attending school, after having broken up with Connell, he 'entered a period of low spirits' (NP, p. 73). About a month later, at a house party, he has sex with an older woman, which makes him feel so bad that he becomes sick. 'There was no one he could talk to about *that*. He was excruciatingly lonely' (NP, p. 74, emphasis added). Even though the narrative is vague about what 'that' refers to, it can be assumed that it is not the fact that he had sex with a 23-year-old woman that he wanted to talk about with his friends. Based on the discussion earlier, this would have been reason for his friends to celebrate. Rather, it can be assumed that 'that' refers to what has happened between him and Marianne and how he feels about it. Connell, who is considered to be a very popular boy by many in his school, finds himself being truly lonely, without anyone to share his pain with. This is further confirmed in the latter part of the novel when, while speaking to a therapist, he explains that he wanted to leave his hometown in the hopes that he would be able to find people to fit in with. 'You know, we were eighteen or whatever, we all acted like idiots. But I guess I found that stuff a bit alienating. . . . I probably thought if I moved here I would fit in better, he says' (NP, p. 217). Connell clearly expresses that knowing 'how to behave' (NP, p. 212) does not mean that he feels in accord with this, nor that the relationships that are afforded to him because of his knowing how to behave are in any way meaningful to him. Arguably, Connell's relation with his peers illustrates Goffman's (1959) theory on identity management. Using theatre as a metaphor, Goffman argues that people are so invested in being accepted by their social circle (the audience at the front of the stage), that they their social identity (created at the backstage) does not necessarily match their true identity. Rather, it is created in a way that conforms to the norms imposed by them (the audience). It is through the adjustment of one's performance to the audience's reactions that social behaviours are defined as appropriate and accepted (Klein, Spears and Reicher, 2007). This is not to be confused with self-presentation, though. Being accepted, in this instance, is more than just a personal goal. '[S]ocial identity performance considers the situations where the actor defines themselves as a group member and performs as such when they think they are visible to an audience' (Sepahpour-Fard *et al.*, 2023, p. 2). Connell's social performance, that is, him knowing 'how to behave' (NP, p. 212), illustrates not only what kind of behaviour is accepted by his peers; rather, it exemplifies the kind of behaviour that enables one to become part of a social group. In other words, Connell's performative superficiality is the only way he can engage in homosocial relations with his male peers, which, however, are far from meaningful, substantial, or significant for him. Indeed, the following chapter focuses on Connell's years at university and the ways in which male homosocial relationships become even more complex while men maturate into adulthood.

References

Anderson, E. (2014) *21st century jocks: Sporting men and contemporary heterosexuality.* Basingstoke: Palgrave Macmillan.

Benenson, J. F. (2013) 'The development of human female competition: Allies and adversaries', *Philosophical Transactions of the Royal Society B: Biological Sciences*, 368(1631), pp. 1–11. https://doi.org/10.1098/rstb.2013.0079.

Bolton, R., Edwards, C., Leane, M., Ó Súilleabháin, F. and Fennell, C. (2022) ' "They're you know, their audience": How women are (ab)used to cement the heterosexual bonds between men', *Irish Journal of Sociology*, 30(1), pp. 3–24. https://doi.org/10.1177/07916035211034355.

Bridges, T. and Pascoe, C. J. (2014) 'Hybrid masculinities: New directions in the sociology of men and masculinities', *Sociology Compass*, 8(3), pp. 246–258. https://doi.org/10.1111/soc4.12134.

Connell, R. W. (1995) *Masculinities.* Berkeley: University of California Press.

Curry, T. (2000) 'Booze and bar fights: A journey to the dark side of college athletics', in J. McKay, M. Messner and D. Sabo (eds.) *Masculinities, gender relations and sport.* London: Sage, pp. 162–175.

Ging, D. (2017) 'Alphas, betas, and incels: Theorizing the masculinities of the manosphere', *Men and Masculinities*, 22(4), pp. 638–657. https://doi.org/10.1177/1097184X17706401.

Goffman, E. (1959) *The presentation of self in everyday life.* New York: Anchor.

Haywood, C., Johansson, T., Hammarén, N., Herz, M. and Ottemo, A. (2017) *The conundrum of masculinity: Hegemony, homosociality, homophobia and heteronormativity.* New York: Routledge.

Holland, J., Ramazanoglu, C., Sharpe, S. and Thomson, R. (2004) *The male in the head: Young people, heterosexuality, and power.* London: The Tufnell Press.

Hruschka, D. J. (2010) 'Friendship: Childhood to adulthood', in D. Hruschka (ed.) *Friendship: Development, ecology, and evolution of a relationship.* Berkeley: University of California Press, pp. 121–145. https://doi.org/10.1525/california/9780520265462.003.0006.

Ibson, J. (2002) *Picturing men: A century of male relationships in everyday American photography.* Chicago: University of Chicago Press.

Klein, O., Spears, R. and Reicher, S. (2007) 'Social identity performance: Extending the strategic side of side', *Personality and Social Psychology Review*, 11(1), pp. 28–45. https://doi.org/10.1177/1088868306294588.

McCormack, M. (2012) *The declining significance of homophobia: How teenage boys are redefining masculinity and heterosexuality.* Oxford: Oxford University Press.

McCormack, M. and Anderson, E. (2014) 'The influence of declining homophobia on men's gender in the United States: An argument for the study of homohysteria', *Sex Roles*, 71(3–4), pp. 109–120. https://doi.org/10.1007/s11199-014-0358-8.

McGuffey, C. S. and Rich, B. L. (1999) 'Playing in the gender transgression zone: Race, class, and hegemonic masculinity in middle childhood', *Gender and Society*, 13(5), pp. 608–627.

Messerschmidt, J. W. (2018) *Hegemonic masculinity.* London: Rowman & Littlefield.

Messner, M. A. (2004) 'On patriarchs and losers: Rethinking men's interests', *Berkeley Journal of Sociology*, 48, pp. 74–88.

Morin, S. F. and Garfinkle, E. M. (1978) 'Male homophobia', *Journal of Social Issues*, 34(1), pp. 29–47. https://doi.org/10.1111/j.1540-4560.1978.tb02539.x.

Oransky, M. and Marecek, J. (2009) ' "I'm not going to be a girl": Masculinity and emotions in boys' friendships and peer groups', *Journal of Adolescent Research*, 24(2), pp. 218–241. https://doi.org/10.1177/0743558408329951.

Pascoe, C. J. (2011) *Dude, you're a fag: Masculinity and sexuality in high school*. Berkeley: University of California Press.

Rich, A. (1980) 'Compulsory heterosexuality and lesbian existence', *Signs*, 5(4), pp. 631–660.

Robinson, S., Anderson, E. and White, A. (2018) 'The bromance: Undergraduate male friendships and the expansion of contemporary homosocial boundaries', *Sex Roles*, 78(1), pp. 94–106. https://doi.org/10.1007/s11199-017-0768-5.

Rooney, S. (2017) *Conversations with friends*. London: Faber & Faber.

Rooney, S. (2018) *Normal people*. London: Faber & Faber.

Schippers, M. (2007) 'Recovering the feminine other: Masculinity, femininity, and gender hegemony', *Theory and Society*, 36(1), pp. 85–102.

Schwalbe, M. (2014) *Manhood acts: Gender and the practices of domination*. Boulder: Paradigm Publishers.

Sepahpour-Fard, M., Quayle, M., Schuld, M. and Yasseri, T. (2023) 'How does the audience affect the way we express our gender roles?' *arXiv*. Available at: http://arxiv.org/abs/2303.12759.

Short, D. (2013) *"Don't be so gay!": Queers, bullying, and making schools safe*. Vancouver: UBC Press.

Thomas, R. J. (2019) 'Sources of friendship and structurally induced homophily across the life course', *Sociological Perspectives*, 62(6), pp. 822–843. https://doi.org/10.1177/0731121419828399.

Vigil, J. M. (2007) 'Asymmetries in the friendship preferences and social styles of men and women', *Human Nature*, 18(2), pp. 143–161. https://doi.org/10.1007/s12110-007-9003-3.

3 Antagonistic and Affectionate-but-Invisible Male Homosociality

Focusing on *Normal People*, the previous chapter examines how teenagers are socialised into what is acceptable and what is not with regard to male homosociality. This chapter also focuses on male homosocial relations in *Normal People*, but its emphasis is on the characters' adult years, especially their time at university. Doing so allows for a more nuanced exploration of the ways in which homosocial relationships intersect with other processes such as social inequalities and gendered hierarchies. The chapter first addresses the role of social class and socioeconomic status in shaping the dynamics of homosocial relations and continues with an exploration of the positive potential of homosociality for young men, with attention to its benefits in relation to mental and emotional health. The chapter concludes with a consideration of male homosocial relationships as seemingly plausible on the condition that they remain invisible. The chapter illustrates conflicting homosociality through the antagonistic homosocial relationships Connell has with Gareth and Jamie and affectionate homosociality through his relationship with Niall. The main argument put forward in the chapter is that social norms around masculinity and masculine behaviour mandate public exhibits of conflicting homosociality whereby men exert their dominance over one another, but when it comes to affectionate homosociality, such public performances are less encouraged, if not discouraged altogether, irrespective of whether they take place in private or not.

A central theme in Rooney's works is class and privilege awareness and the role of social class and privilege in establishing and maintaining relationships, particularly in the way it becomes an impediment for some and affords opportunities for others (Barros-Del Río, 2022, p. 183). Connell moves to Dublin to study at Trinity College, which many consider to be the most prestigious and elite university both in terms of quality and in terms of student demographics (Courtois, 2018, pp. 132–133). In doing so, he finds himself socialising with new people, and he appears to be so self-aware of how others view him in relation to his social class and his rural background that he becomes almost unable to process and participate in initial interactions with his classmates, especially male ones. When he finds himself interacting with new people, he appears self-conscious about the socioeconomic differences between himself

DOI: 10.4324/9781032644974-4

and most of his peers, irrespective of whether such differences are indeed highlighted by them or not (Carregal-Romero, 2023, p. 228). For example, at Gareth's party, Connell appears to interpret Gareth's comments to him as commentary about Connell's working-class background. 'Good to see you, man, says Gareth. Good to see you. I like the backpack, very nineties' (NP, p. 66). If this was intended to be compliment, Connell does not appear to interpret it as one. 'Connell had a six-pack of cider with him, but he's reluctant to do anything that would draw attention to his backpack, in case Gareth might feel prompted to comment on it further' (NP, p. 67). Connell's reaction does not come across as very coherent in response to what appears to be a legitimate effort on Gareth's side to be welcoming and helpful. Rather, Connell seems to be calculating whether Gareth's behaviour is a genuine attempt to accommodate Connell or a volitional yet fiendish way of calling Connell out for not belonging there. When Gareth asks Connell if a bottle of Corona would be ok for him, 'Connell looks at him for a second, wondering if the question is ironic or genuinely servile' (NP, p. 67). At this stage in the novel, it becomes unclear whether Connell is self-conscious in relation to differences between his socioeconomic background and this of his classmates or in relation to how he believes others to perceive him coming from a rural background. However, his ongoing questioning of Gareth's motives is not unwarranted. Since moving to Dublin, Connell has been made fun of because of his rural background. 'In the Workmans the other night, Connell told a girl he was from Sligo and she made a funny face and said: Yeah, you look like it' (NP, p. 69). In addition to comments such as this one, Connell is becoming increasingly aware of differences between himself and his classmates.

> All the guys in his class wear the same waxed hunting jackets and plum-coloured chinos, not that Connell has a problem with people dressing how they want, but he would feel like a complete prick wearing that stuff. At the same time, it forces him to acknowledge that his own clothes are cheap and unfashionable. His only shoes are an ancient pair of Adidas trainers, which he wears everywhere, even to the gym.
>
> (NP, p. 70)

Even though these observations are somewhat factual in that Connell's background and current financial situation are significantly different to that of most of his classmates, the novel does not present this as a negative contributing factor to how others, or who, interact with Connell. That means that those who are not of similar socioeconomic or rural background as Connell cannot understand his behaviour, nor can they realise what impact such difference might have on him, resulting in even more prominent distance between Connell and his peers. During the rest of the party scene, for example, Gareth seems to be genuinely interested in getting to know Connell, maintaining small talk, trying to make him feel comfortable, and introducing him to his girlfriend who, ironically, is Marianne (NP, pp. 71–72). What is of interest here is that for the other characters, Connell's anxiety in relation to class-related or background-related differences between himself and his peers does not appear to punctuate the friendships he can potentially establish with other people, especially men. However, it should not go unnoticed that in the dynamic between the two men, it is Connell who is aware of class and social background differences, not Gareth, possibly nodding to the inherent unevenness of this relationship whereby the person who comes from a lower social class or less privileged background is bound to frame his friendships in light of such differences, while the one who comes from an upper class or more privileged background is less aware, or completely oblivious, to such differences.

Empirical research on the effects of differences in social class and male homosociality suggests that men who come from upper classes are not only aware but they also find opportunities to make public displays of their class background when interacting with men of working classes as a way of confirming their dominance (Arxer, 2011, p. 409). That is, one way for someone to enact dominant masculinity is through engaging in a homosocial relationship with someone else of lower social class and making their socioeconomic differences prominent. However, Gareth's behaviour toward Connell is not consistent with Arxer's (2011) findings in that he does not appear to be stressing any fact about himself that would highlight any class differences between Connell and him. Instead, he comes across as accommodating, interested in getting to know Connell and helping him network with other students. Álvarez-Rivadulla *et al.* (2022, p. 665), reporting on a study exploring cross-class friendships in a university setting, argue that, with the exception of people coming from the elite classes, university students are likely to engage in cross-class friendships whereby people from upper classes often act as mediators in integrating those of lower classes with the rest of the student population. Even though we are never presented with Gareth's exact socioeconomic situation, it becomes clear that he is at a better socioeconomic standing than Connell, and his behaviour is in concert with the findings of Álvarez-Rivadulla *et al.* (2022). In the dynamic between Gareth and Connell, it is the behaviour of the latter that is surprising at first, given how defensive he is toward Gareth and misinterpreting everything Gareth says or asks as an attack or an ironic comment about Connell's background. In an attempt to discuss the dynamic ways in which homosociality is enacted, Kariotis (2016, p. 74) uses the terms conflictual and collaborative homosociality. This distinction can not only describe the attitudes of two different people when engaging in a homosocial relationship, in this case Gareth exhibiting collaborative and Connell conflictual homosociality; these can also be used as analytical tools describing the complexity of homosocial relationships and accounting for intersectional issues that can inform, if not affect, a homosocial bond. To illustrate,

Connell finds himself in the peculiar position whereby he pushes himself to meet new people and network while being defensive, assuming that people are constantly judging his background. It follows that Connell exhibits both collaborative and conflictual homosociality in his interactions with Gareth. It can be argued that collaborative homosociality emerges from what Collins and Sroufe (1999, p. 132) describe as an enhanced desire to form intimate friendships as a scaffolding step toward family independence. Similarly, conflictual homosociality can be attributed to Connell's experience, a kind of imposter syndrome as discussed by Ali *et al.* (2019, p. 100) whereby students, of any level, who come from lower socioeconomic backgrounds struggle when they find themselves in educational settings that are traditionally considered prestigious, believing that they do not belong there. Connell's behaviour in the short exchange he has with Gareth is significant in that it allows for a novel understanding of homosocial relationships between men, one that does not focus on how upper classes exert gendered dominance based on their high socioeconomic standing; rather, a new approach to the study of intersectionality and homosociality becomes possible, one that focuses on the complex ways in which men who are not part of the upper classes navigate and negotiate their homosocial relationships with other men.

The extent to which Connell frames most of his relationships, at least in their initial stages, through the prism of class difference is evident not only in the exchanges he has with Gareth; similar incidents are observed when Connell interacts with other people as well. For instance, one night he calls Marianne, explains that he has been mugged in Dun Laoghaire, an area outside Dublin, and asks her to lend him some money to pay the taxi that will bring him back to his apartment. When he arrives at her place and sees that her friends are there with her, he appears to default to presuming people would ridicule him for coming from a different socioeconomic background to theirs. 'Fucking lowlife scum, says Jamie. Who me? Connell says. That's not very nice. We can't all go to private school, you know. . . . I was talking about the guy that robbed you, says Jamie' (NP, p. 145). In this exchange, it becomes apparent that Connell's first instinct is to interpret negative comments as if they are directed to him, and he is ready to assume a defensive role, justifying an inferiority that he seems to believe others attribute to him. Connell's relationship with Jamie is more complicated than two male acquaintances because of their mutual interest in Marianne. Even when they first meet, Connell and Jamie do not interact much. Instead, they engage in a game of pool where they do not talk to one another; rather, they externalise any joust they might have with one another through pocketing balls while their friends, Marianne included, are watching them (NP, p. 90). Almost all the exchanges between the two men that follow in the novel are of similar quality; that is, they antagonise each other continuously and in a public manner, stressing thus each one's need to be regarded by others as being better than the other one. In the scene where Connell is at Marianne's apartment after having been robbed, for instance, they engage in a short debate over people addicted to drugs. Jamie says,

> he was probably stealing to buy drugs, by the way, that's what most of them do. . . . Oh well, he [Connell] says. It's not an easy life out there for a drug addict. . . . They could always try, I don't know, giving up drugs? says Jamie. Connell laughs and says: Yeah, I'm sure they've just never thought of that.
>
> (NP, p. 145)

The context in which this exchange is taking place suggests that the purpose of this short discussion is not a genuine exchange of perspectives; rather, it seems more as an excuse for Connell to throw cold water on any admiration people, especially Marianne, might have for Jamie. Connell is drunk, bleeding after having been beaten and robbed, and in need of some money to get back home. Having such an argument in that moment only confirms the rivalry between the two men. The incident has many similarities to the one between Connell and Gareth described earlier. Connell assumes that people of higher socioeconomic standing to his attempt to belittle him by reminding him of his lower background, while Gareth and Jamie – both of higher socioeconomic standing – are ignorant as to how Connell might feel or interpret what they say to him.

Connell's public displays of loathing toward Jamie can be understood as exemplifications of what Eisenstein (1978, p. 21) terms 'capitalist patriarchy' to describe the impossibility of understanding the one without the other: capitalism without patriarchy and patriarchy without capitalism given that they 'embody relations of power' which enable the two systems to reinforce one another. To illustrate this further, the dynamic between Connell and Jamie is defined by their socioeconomic differences as well as their mutual interest in Marianne, with the latter reinforcing the former. That is, their gendered antagonism over Marianne reinforces and accentuates their socioeconomic differences and *vice versa*. A comparison between Connell's interaction with Gareth and his interaction with Jamie provides important relevant insights. In the scene at Gareth's party that is described at the beginning of this chapter, Connell is defensive, assuming Gareth is being haughty toward him. At that point, Connell is not aware of Gareth's relationship with Marianne. In contrast, when Connell interacts with Jamie, he does not come across as defensive; rather, he appears to be more self-confident, if not aggressive toward Jamie. Notwithstanding the fact that he might genuinely dislike Jamie, the fact that Marianne is a variable in the dynamic between the two young men cannot be overlooked. For example, during the first interaction between Connell and Jamie at the pool game, Connell appears to be more antagonistic toward Jamie, possibly as a way to appear confident in front of Marianne and to enact dominant masculinity in front of Jamie. Kimmel (1997, p. 239) explains that, through competition, men attempt to assert their dominance over other men, and in doing so, they affirm their manliness to themselves, the other men, and anyone who witnesses the conflict. The second time the two men interact, when Connell visits Marianne to borrow money after having been robbed, their situation is reversed in that Jamie is Marianne's new boyfriend. In both instances, Connell and Jamie have more than their socioeconomic background to separate them; they are also competing for the same woman. Mansfield (2007, p. 58) explains that patriarchy demands men to performatively assert their manliness continuously, especially in the presence of other men. A way to do so is by negotiating a relationship of dominance. In the example of Connell and Jamie at Marianne's house, Connell is seen to provoke Jamie to express his arguably elitist ideas in front of others and possibly lose their respect, especially Marianne's. In this instance, the two men are not only engaged in a gender-based antagonism, competing over their manliness; rather, they also antagonise each other over their socioeconomic background and how it has shaped how they view and navigate life more generally. As such, it appears that class and patriarchy reinforce one another and inform the way men relate to one another.

Indeed, the dynamic between class and patriarchy invites, at least, a consideration of the interplay between the two systems in the ways male homosocial relationships are structured (Hart, 2016). This is further illustrated through the dynamic between Connell and Jamie, especially when they are in Italy. During this time, Jamie is still with Marianne, but the more Connell interacts with her, the more Jamie appears to become insecure around Connell because of Connell's relationship with Marianne both as ex-partners and as people who know and understand each other intimately. Perhaps for this reason, the interactions between the two men in the novel, not only during their time in Italy, are very rare and superficial. When Connell arrives in Italy at Marianne's family villa and sees Jamie, their greeting is short and clearly signals the dislike they have for one another. 'Connell makes a half-nodding gesture, just barely inclining his chin upwards. Jamie gives him a mocking smile and says: You're looking rough, mate' (NP, pp. 162–163). The narrator further confirms that 'Jamie has been a continual object of loathing and derision for Connell since he became Marianne's boyfriend' (NP, pp. 163). Indeed, Connell's wordless greeting to Jamie suggests that he does not want to put any effort in establishing some sort of relationship with Jamie. From their previous interactions, it becomes clear that the two men are very different and would very likely not have had any interactions had Jamie not been Marianne's boyfriend. What is interesting, though, is Jamie's response to Connell in this short exchange where, instead of welcoming him or returning the nodding gesture, he chooses to make a belittling comment about Connell's appearance in front of everyone else, suggesting his need to remind Connell of his position in an imaginary hierarchy between the two, confirming Kimmel (1997, p. 239) and Mansfield's (2007, p. 58) arguments about the need of men to assert their manliness over other men by making themselves appear to be better than other men. Additionally, his comment about Connell's appearance is ambivalent in that it could be a gender-related attack, a class-related attack, or both. It is possible that for Jamie, Connell's appearance could have been a result of Connell not being tough enough for such a physically demanding trip (gender-related attack) and/or not having enough money to afford himself more stops and better clothes (class-related attack). Jamie's provoking of Connell continues when, during an argument between Jamie and Marianne in the kitchen of the villa, Connell goes to check on Marianne, interrupting the argument and making his presence known to Jamie so that the situation does not escalate any further. Upon seeing Connell in the kitchen, Jamie drops emphatically one of the glasses they have been using to drink champagne to the floor. Earlier, he was told that these glasses are of emotional significance for Marianne because they belonged to her father (NP, p. 171). The fact that he decides to destroy one of the glasses only when Connell enters the room can be interpreted as another way for Jamie to provoke Connell to engage in some sort of reaction, only this time Jamie does it indirectly by hurting Marianne's feelings in front of Connell (NP, p. 178). Similar to the previous incident, this incident further illustrates Eisenstein's (1978, p. 21) encouragement to consider the intersections of gender and class when analysing men's relationships with other men. In this moment, Jamie provokes Connell by highlighting his higher socioeconomic status which affords him to believe that he is entitled to act in any way he likes without considering the repercussions of his actions. At the same time, in this incident, Jamie also asserts his manliness by reminding both Marianne and Connell that Marianne is his and so are her material possessions.

Jamie's attitude toward Connell also seems to be driven by expectations people living in urban centres have with regard to expected behaviours of men who live, or come from, rural areas. There have been numerous empirical studies confirming a discord between popular expectations and lived experiences of rural masculinities. With specific attention to violence, Carrington *et al.* (2013, p. 19) explain that people who do not come from or have lived in rural areas stereotypically believe rural men to engage in public acts of violence, such as engaging in pub fights. However, their findings suggest that rural men are more likely to engage in acts of internalised violence, that is self-harm, than being violent toward other men. Indeed, there is an array of empirical studies noting a changing pattern associated with rural masculinities, with particular attention to the changing ways in which men perform masculinities in rural settings (Laoire, 2001, 2002; Bye, 2009; Pini and Mayers, 2019; Thompson, 2021). These studies note that men in rural societies engage in softer displays of masculinity than the rough and tough stereotype people in urban environments seem to associate with them. Jamie's behaviour toward Connell seems to illustrate such stereotypical expectations urban people hold. By continuously provoking Connell to engage in some act of violence or another, Jamie seems to want to ensure that his peers, primarily Marianne who is also from a rural location, are reminded of why Connell is different and should not be embraced by them. At the same time, Jamie enacts dominant masculinity which, he seems to believe, is justified on the basis of his urban background. That is, for Jamie, the only exhibit of a dominant masculine order he can use to shift the dynamic between him and Connell is his urban upbringing which he seems to believe is superior to Connell's rural background. Most recently, Gater's (2023) ethnographic research further confirms that popular beliefs about an assumed inferiority of lower and working-class masculinities, including rural masculinities, on the basis of 'homophobia, sexism, suppression of emotion and avoidance of physical tactility' or indeed traditional notions of the uncultured man are found to be unwarranted. Gater's findings highlight a change in the ways masculinity is performed in non-privileged settings, with softer approaches to masculine behaviour becoming more common. Following on from the earlier discussion about socioeconomic background and masculinity, it becomes apparent that male homosociality is a complex and intersectional process whereby identity markers are negotiated and used continuously in establishing a power dynamic that will benefit one and hurt the other. That is, what has been discussed as hegemonic masculinity and men's engagement in positioning themselves as high as possible in a hierarchy of masculinities is more complex because it involves more than just gender qualities. In Jamie and Connell's relationship, for example, masculine traits as such are rarely addressed; rather, class and socioeconomic background are operationalised as if they were markers of who is the better man.

An antipodal relationship to the one Connell has with Jamie is the one he has with Niall. Their interactions are few and far between, but it becomes clear that they genuinely care for one another and allow themselves to be open and vulnerable with one another even. What is of interest in comparing the two relationships is that in both instances, Connell is the outsider to the city, while Jamie and Niall are not. However, the relationship between Connell and Jamie and the one between Connell and Niall differ significantly. For instance, a week before the end of spring term, Connell's boss decides to reduce Connell's hours at work, which would leave Connell with just enough to cover rent. The most sensible decision for him is to leave his Dublin room and spend the summer at his mother's house. Indeed, Connell decides to do so, and when he announces this to Niall, the response he got was one of concern about himself and his relationship with Marianne instead of focusing on the uncomfortable situation of having to find another roommate or not caring for how this would affect Connell in the first place. 'Niall was very nice about it, said the room would still be there for him in September and all of that. What about yourself and Marianne? Niall asked. And Connell said: Yeah, yeah. I don't know. I haven't told her yet' (NP, p. 122). Up until that point in the novel, there has never been any particular attention to the friendship between the two young men. As such, Niall's reaction to Connell's news signifies not only that the two of them have formed a close friendship but also the possibility of a healthy and meaningful relationship between two young men. Additionally, considering the socioeconomic context within which the story takes place intensifies this observation. *Normal People* is set in the post-Celtic Tiger years where a severe housing crisis followed Ireland's entering a bailout programme that severely affected the economy of the country (Lima, 2021, p. 3283). Niall would have no trouble having a short-term tenant for the summer, though the narrative is not clear as to whether he is planning to do so or not. He could also avoid the trouble of renting it short-term and then giving it back to Connell by finding another long-term tenant to replace Connell. However, his decision to keep the room for Connell to return to when the next academic year starts is an instantaneous one, suggesting that he cares both about maintaining his friendship with him and about helping him during this difficult time. Further, the fact that his first question is about how this decision will affect Connell's relationship with Marianne signifies that the friendship between the two men is not a superficial one; rather, Niall shows that he cares enough about Connell to understand that such a decision might impact Connell's relationship with Marianne and, expressing his concern, encourages Connell to discuss this with him should he wish to do so.

The relationship between Connell and Niall illustrates what recent research on homosociality and masculinities suggests: young heterosexual men are likely to form strong bonds based on emotional connection. Notable recent examples include Anderson and McCormack's (2018) theorisation of the stigmatisation of homophobia as a significant reason contributing to changing attitudes toward homosociality and Robinson and Anderson's (2022) recent study on the bromance. Both studies provide observations of a changing attitude toward the ways in which male homosociality is performed, including direct, verbal, and/or indirect expressions of love and caring. Anderson (2009, p. 151) further argues that such expressions of homosocial intimacy are encouraged in societies and cultures that exhibit reduced levels of homophobia which, in turn, enables heterosexual men to engage in intimate friendships with one another without the fear of being considered to be homosexuals and consequently suffer discrimination and social exclusion. Such very intimate relationships between men are described as 'bromance', that is, a 'close and intimate nonsexual and homosocial relationship between two (or more) men' (Hammarén and Johansson, 2014, p. 6) which resembles the closeness, honesty, and authenticity of the relation between two brothers who, in the case of the bromance, chose one another (Robinson and Anderson, 2022, pp. 99–100). From the very few interactions that are presented in the novel, it becomes apparent that Connell and Niall are very close. Niall understands the financial struggles Connell experiences, knows his feelings for Marianne, and shows a very in-depth understanding of the dynamic of the relationship between Connell and Marianne. When Connell tells him that he will have to leave for the summer, Niall's immediate response is to ask about Marianne, showing that he understands the significance of proximity and physical contact for Connell and Marianne. Additionally, he overlooks his own interest in favour of accommodating Connell during a time of need when he reassures him that he will keep the room for him instead of renting it out and making some profit. Niall's selflessness in this moment is illustrative of a very close friendship, possibly even a bromance, between the two young men, suggesting that intimate homosociality might indeed be possible. It becomes clear from this, as well as from the interactions between the two men that are discussed later, that their relation is not based on reciprocity; we never observe Connell supporting or helping Niall emotionally – without this to mean that this does not happen. Even though reciprocity is considered to be a significant determining factor for the maintenance of a friendship (Requena, 1995, p. 272), it is less important in instances of bromances (Robinson, White and Anderson, 2019, p. 864). That is, the fact that Connell does not appear, at least in the events covered in the novel, to be reciprocating the attention and care he received from Niall seems to have little to no effect on the quality of their relationship.

Another case in point punctuating the possibility of a meaningful bond between two men is observed toward the end of the book where Connell is struggling with his mental health following the suicide of his high school classmate and friend, Rob. Through analepses, it becomes clear that Connell suffered a serious mental health breakdown after finding out about Rob, and Connell spends almost three months trying to come to terms with it. After it becomes clear that Connell is in the waiting room of a counselling service, the narrator explains that Connell is there following Niall's suggestion. 'It was Niall who told him about the service. What he said specifically was: It's free, so you might as well. Niall is a practical person, and he shows compassion in practical ways' (NP, p. 201). There are three significant points that warrant attention in this short passage. Firstly, Niall's concern and interest about Connell's well-being becomes apparent despite, as we find out later, that they no longer share the same apartment since Connell lives in his scholarship accommodation. That is, the bond between the two is not dependent on being roommates; rather, they continue caring for one another even when they do not live together. Secondly, it is important to note that Connell followed Niall's suggestion and visited the counselling service. Building on findings from previous studies, Cole and Ingram (2020, p. 441) confirm that men are likely to avoid asking for psychological help not only as a result of self-stigmatisation but also out of fear of breaking norms associated with masculinity and gender role expectations. However, Connell's acceptance of Niall's advice provides a positive contribution of homosociality to men's mental health. It is because of the relationship Connell and Niall have built over the course of their time in Dublin that Connell trusts and follows Niall's advice which, as it unfolds later in the novel, has very positive effects on Connell's mental health. The third significant point to note from this passage, though, is the narrator's remark about Niall being a 'practical person' who 'shows compassion in practical ways' (NP, p. 201). What is interesting in this remark is the apparent need to hedge Niall's concern toward Connell, making it clear that Niall's compassion is not expressed through emotional vulnerability or connection with Connell, but through pragmatic suggestions that can have an immediate benefit for Connell who follows suit. However, defining Niall's compassionate nature in terms of practicality can be understood as an attempt to preserve certain expectations regarding masculinity and male homosociality in that men can indeed be helpful toward one another on the proviso that such help is strictly of practical nature whereby emotional support is not something that one man can offer to another, but they can direct one toward finding the help or support they need elsewhere.

Men have been traditionally subjected to cultural norms and expectations that restrict their ability to relate to their affect and reduce the likelihood of them admitting to be struggling mentally and/or emotionally (Fehr, 1995, p. 127). Empirical studies confirm young men's inability to understand, let alone discuss with others, their own emotions due to what Scourfield (2005, p. 40) calls 'emotional illiteracy', an effect of hegemonic masculinity that not only limits but also directs men away from any possible attempt to develop an emotional reserve that can help them cope with life. Cleary (2012) conducted a study among university male students confirming expectations about masculine behaviour to be the reason participants of the study cited for feeling unable to discuss their mental health struggles with their friends (p. 504). What is particularly distressing about the findings of Cleary's (2012) study is that some of the young men who participated in the study reported that they had attempted suicide as a result of their inability to reach out to a friend and ask for help. Silva (2015) and Robinson and Anderson (2022) highlight the significance of male homosocial relations for preventing men from reaching a breaking point whereby their presumed inability to share their emotional and mental anxieties with others might either put a strain on their already-encumbered mental and/or emotional health or encourage them to engage in self-harming behaviours. Their research supports that when men engage in close friendships with other men and overcome societal restrictions attached to masculinity, their mental and emotional health benefits overall either from having someone to unload or by receiving encouragement to ask for professional help. Indeed, in the case of Connell and Niall's relationship, it becomes clear that Connell makes the decision to visit a specialist and receive professional help only after Niall advises him to do so. Even though the friendship between the two men is not punctuated a lot in the novel, it is in significant moments like Connell's mental struggle that the significance of Niall's friendship is witnessed. What is particularly interesting in the relationship of the two men is that not only does Niall care and support Connell but he seems to know exactly how to do so, suggesting that the two of them do not have a superficial friendship, but one whereby they understand what each other needs and what the best way to provide them with it might be. The benefits of this kind of friendship for the mental and emotional health of the men who form part of it provides a potential to escape the inevitable detrimental effects emotional repression is reported to have had on the well-being of men (Emslie *et al.*, 2007). In particular, not only is the possibility of male homosociality challenging the constraining limitations of normative expectations about masculine behaviour illustrated through Connell and Niall's relationship but, also, the crucial contribution of homosociality to men's mental and emotional health is highlighted in a manner that might encourage readers, especially young men, to re-evaluate their attitudes toward friendships with other men in light of how traditional expectations about masculinity can and ought to be challenged collectively through honest and intimate friendships with other men.

However, despite the benefits of this relationship for the two men, the way their friendship is presented in the novel further confirms the main argument of this dissertation: in Rooney's novels, male homosociality, even in its rare occurrences, *appears to be* impossible. Indeed, the instances where Connell and Niall's relationship is presented are rare. However, it quickly becomes clear that Niall's friendship provides Connell with significant support, not only in relation to his mental health, as was discussed earlier, but in less significant ways, such as in advising him how to act in complicated situations. For instance, this is evident when they communicate with their eyes after Marianne and Jamie have an argument at dinner in Marianne's villa in Italy.

> By the time Connell turns his attention back to the table Niall is staring at him. He doesn't know what Niall's stare means. He tries squinting his eyes to show Niall he's confused. Niall casts a significant look at the house and then back at him. Connell looks over his right shoulder.
>
> (NP, pp. 177–178)

Whether Connell would have decided to go and help Marianne in the kitchen during her argument with Jamie without Niall's prompting is not clear; what is clear, though, is Niall's attentive, almost brotherly, behaviour toward Connell. The two of them appear to be sharing more time than is presented in the novel. At an earlier moment, when Marianne and Connell admit their relationship to Peggy, and Marianne asks Connell if he has a problem telling people about them, Connell suggests that he has been talking to Niall about Marianne a lot. 'Marianne asked him once if he was 'ashamed' of her but she was just joking. That's funny, he said. Niall thinks I brag about you too much' (NP, p. 93, emphasis in original). What is interesting about this remark is that there is no point in the novel where Connell can be witnessed bragging about Marianne to Niall or discussing any of his personal matters with him. It is also interesting that bragging is not something that Connell is ever seen doing in the novel. Actually, as the previous chapter illustrates, during their time in high school, Marianne complains about Connell's friends who 'brag' about their sexual encounters (NP, p.14), exaggerating their accomplishments to show – or assume – some kind of superiority over others. Most likely, Niall's remark refers to Connell expressing his pride in Marianne being his girlfriend without the negative connotations that are typically associated with bragging. On the one hand, the fact that Connell communicates these feelings to Niall highlights the importance of male homosociality for men, especially young men, in creating a safe space where they can express themselves, their interests, and desires.

At the same time, though, the fact that these moments are never captured in the novel further highlights an underlying societal expectation about male friendship: that it needs to be protected from public display no matter how intimate and strong it might be.

Robinson and Anderson (2022) confirm that, contrary to traditional understandings of societal expectations of masculinity and the subsequent restrictions they impose on male homosociality, young men report engaging in very close friendships with other men, such as bromances, and benefitting from them. The caveat is that such relationships are observed in contexts where homophobia is generally criticised, which is not to mean that, individually, men who engage in bromances are not homophobic; rather, the context within which they form such friendships does not encourage a homophobic culture irrespective of each individual's attitudes toward homosexuality (Robinson, Anderson and White, 2018). Chen (2012, p. 262) further confirms the significance of lack of societal control over gender and sexuality for intimate male friendships to flourish, but also finds bromances to be inherently heteronormative (p. 249) in that the 'bro' part of the bromance is meant to be understood as not gay. As such, despite bromances, or any forms of intimate male friendship, providing men with an opportunity to challenge traditional norms of masculinity and contributing to their overall well-being – and arguably the well-being of society at large for that matter – they are also markers of societal control in that their public expression is dependent on societal attitudes about gender and sexuality. The chapter has shown that male homosociality is a complex structure, the understanding of which requires intersectional approaches such as the role of the individual men's socioeconomic background. In discussing Connell's interactions with Gareth and Jamie, the chapter highlights the central role of antagonistic homosocial relations in the maintenance of hegemonic norms around masculinity.

However, the close friendship between Connell and Niall suggests that men can engage in more positive, affectionate homosocial relations. Though, despite the fact that there are possibilities for men to engage in very close friendships with each other, these are still heavily policed. In a recent study focusing on same-sex friendship attitudes among young Irish men, O'Dwyer (2022, pp. 30–31) observes that young men are likely to become very close to one another and publicly express such closeness, but only when they find themselves in strictly homosocial environments, such as a sport club; that is, men are found to be policing their own expressions of love and admiration toward other men when they find themselves outside homosocial environments out of fear of being judged and discriminated against for violating societal scripts of expected gendered behaviour. In that sense, homosociality is still very much bound to be invisible, if not impossible. Without arguing that Rooney's decision to conceal aspects or moments of Connell and Niall's friendship, the rarity of their interactions in the novel can illustrate a wider societal directive about male homosocial relations that restricts them not in relation to whether they are allowed to exist or not; rather, it restricts the ways in which such relations become available to the public eye. In that sense, male homosociality does not appear to be impossible *per se*, but it is definitely subject for policing and societal scrutiny whereby two men can be very close friends as long as they do not make a big deal out of it.

References

Ali, S., Yasin, G., Hussain, J. and Zunaira (2019) 'Impact of social class on individual's response to educational process', *Journal of Languages, Culture and Civilization*, 1(2), pp. 93–101. https://doi.org/10.47067/jlcc.v1i2.11.

Álvarez-Rivadulla, M. J., Jaramillo, A. M., Fajardo, F., Cely, L., Molano, A. and Montes, F. (2022) 'College integration and social class', *Higher Education*, 84(3), pp. 647–669. https://doi.org/10.1007/s10734-021-00793-6.

Anderson, E. (2009) *Inclusive masculinities: The changing nature of masculinity.* London: Routledge.

Anderson, E. and McCormack, M. (2018) 'Inclusive masculinity theory: Overview, reflection and refinement', *Journal of Gender Studies*, 27(5), pp. 547–561. https://doi.org/10.1080/09589236.2016.1245605.

Arxer, S. L. (2011) 'Hybrid masculine power: Reconceptualizing the relationship between homosociality and hegemonic masculinity', *Humanity & Society*, 35(4), pp. 390–422. https://doi.org/10.1177/016059761103500404.

Barros-Del Río, M. A. (2022) 'Sally Rooney's normal people: The millennial novel of formation in recessionary Ireland', *Irish Studies Review*, 30(2), pp. 176–192. https://doi.org/10.1080/09670882.2022.2080036.

Bye, L. M. (2009) ' "How to be a rural man": Young men's performances and negotiations of rural masculinities', *Journal of Rural Studies*, 25(3), pp. 278–288. https://doi.org/10.1016/j.jrurstud.2009.03.002.

Carregal-Romero, J. (2023) 'Unspeakable injuries and neoliberal subjectivities in Sally Rooney's conversations with friends and normal people', in M. T. Caneda-Cabrera and J. Carregal-Romero (eds.) *Narratives of the unspoken in contemporary Irish fiction: Silences that speak.* Basingstoke: Palgrave Macmillan, pp. 213–233.

Carrington, K., McIntosh, A., Hogg, R. and Scott, J. (2013) 'Rural masculinities and the internalisation of violence in agricultural communities', *International Journal of Rural Criminology*, 2(1), pp. 3–14. https://doi.org/10.18061/1811/58849.

Chen, E. J. (2012) 'Caught in a bad bromance', *Texas Journal of Women, Gender, and the Law*, 21(2), pp. 241–266.

Cleary, A. (2012) 'Suicidal action, emotional expression, and the performance of masculinities', *Social Science & Medicine*, 74(4), pp. 498–505. https://doi.org/10.1016/j.socscimed.2011.08.002.

Cole, B. P. and Ingram, P. B. (2020) 'Where do I turn for help? Gender role conflict, self-stigma, and college men's help-seeking for depression', *Psychology of Men & Masculinities*, 21(3), pp. 441–452. https://doi.org/10.1037/men0000245.

Collins, W. A. and Sroufe, L. A. (1999) 'Capacity for intimate relationships: A developmental construction', in W. Furman, B. B. Brown and C. Feiring (eds.) *The development of romantic relationships in adolescence.* Cambridge: Cambridge University Press, pp. 125–147. https://doi.org/10.1017/CBO9781316182185.007.

Courtois, A. (2018) 'The global ambitions of Irish universities: Internationalizing practices and emerging stratification in the Irish higher education sector', in R. Bloch, A. Mitterle, C. Paradeise and T. Peter (eds.) *Universities and the production of elites: Discourses, policies, and strategies of excellence and stratification in higher education.* Basingstoke: Palgrave Macmillan, pp. 127–148. https://doi.org/10.1007/978-3-319-53970-6_6.

Eisenstein, Z. R. (ed.) (1978) *Capitalist patriarchy and the case for socialist feminism.* New York: Monthly Review Press.

Emslie, C., Ridge D., Ziebland, S. and Hunt, K. (2007) 'Exploring men's and women's experiences of depression and engagement with health professionals: More similarities than differences? A qualitative interview study', *BMC Family Practice*, 8(1). https://doi.org/10.1186/1471-2296-8-43.

Fehr, B. (1995) *Friendship processes.* Thousand Oaks: Sage.

Gater, R. (2023) 'Amalgamated masculinities: The masculine identity of contemporary marginalised working-class young men', *Sociology.* https://doi.org/10.1177/00380385231172121.

Hammarén, N. and Johansson, T. (2014) 'Homosociality: In between power and intimacy', *Sage Open*, June–March, pp. 1–11. https://doi.org/10.1177/2158244013518057.

Hart, M. (2016) 'Capitalist patriarchy', in *The Wiley Blackwell encyclopedia gender and sexuality studies.* Oxford: Wiley Blackwell. https://doi.org/10.1002/9781118663219.wbegss403.

Kariotis, F. G. (2016) *Between class and friendship: Homosociality in an all-male residence hall in the US.* Central European University. Available at: https://shorturl.at/bgvG6 (Accessed: 15 March 2023).

Kimmel, M. S. (1997) 'Masculinity as homophobia: Fear, shame and silence in the construction of gender identity', in M. M. Gergen and S. N. Davis (eds.) *Toward a new psychology of gender.* Florence, KY: Routledge, pp. 223–242.

Laoire, C. N. (2001) 'A matter of life and death? Men, masculinities and staying "behind" in rural Ireland', *Sociologia Ruralis*, 41(2), pp. 220–236. https://doi.org/10.1111/1467-9523.00179.

Laoire, C. N. (2002) 'Young farmers, masculinities and change in rural Ireland', *Irish Geography*, 35(1), pp. 16–27. https://doi.org/10.1080/00750770209555790.

Lima, V. (2021) 'From housing crisis to housing justice: Towards a radical right to a home', *Urban Studies*, 58(16), pp. 3282–3298. https://doi.org/10.1177/0042098021995128.

Mansfield, H. C. (2007) *Manliness.* New York: Yale University Press.

O'Dwyer, F. (2022) 'The functions of collegial humour in male–only sporting interactions', *Te Reo: The Journal of the Linguistic Society of New Zealand*, 64(2), pp. 15–36.

Pini, B. and Mayers, R. (2019) 'Rural masculinities', in L. Gottzén, U. Mellström and T. Shefer (eds.) *Routledge international handbook of masculinity studies.* London: Routledge, pp. 302–310.

Requena, F. (1995) 'Friendship and subjective well-being in Spain: A cross-national comparison with the United States', *Social Indicators Research*, 35(3), pp. 271–288. https://doi.org/10.1007/BF01079161.

Robinson, S. and Anderson, E. (2022) *Bromance: Male friendship, love and sport.* Basingstoke: Palgrave Macmillan.

Robinson, S., Anderson, E. and White, A. (2018) 'The bromance: Undergraduate male friendships and the expansion of contemporary homosocial boundaries', *Sex Roles*, 78(1), pp. 94–106. https://doi.org/10.1007/s11199-017-0768-5.

Robinson, S., White, A. and Anderson, E. (2019) 'Privileging the bromance: A critical appraisal of romantic and bromantic relationships', *Men and Masculinities*, 22(5), pp. 850–871. https://doi.org/10.1177/1097184X17730386.

Rooney, S. (2018) *Normal people*. London: Faber & Faber.

Scourfield, J. (2005) 'Suicidal masculinities', *Sociological Research Online*, 10(2), pp. 35–44. https://doi.org/10.5153/sro.1057.

Silva, J. M. (2015) *Coming up short: Working-class adulthood in an age of uncertainty.* Oxford: Oxford University Press.

Thompson, E. H. (2021) 'Rural masculinities', in L. Kaye (ed.) *Handbook of rural aging.* New York: Routledge, pp. 279–283.

4 Making Male Homosociality Possible?

Unlike Rooney's first two novels, *Beautiful World, Where Are You* portrays men's homosocial relationships in much more detail, allowing for a closer exploration of how dynamics between men are formed and the significance such bonds may have for them. The previous chapter, focusing on *Normal People* and the relationship between Connell and Niall, concludes with a consideration of homosocial relationships as possible but invisible. However, in *Beautiful World, Where Are You*, Rooney devotes a considerable amount of time and space in detailing the possibility of homosociality between Felix and Simon. In doing so, the need for such relationships and the benefits they offer to the men engaged in them is highlighted, as is an optimistic outlook in relation to contemporary masculinities. The chapter opens with a consideration of brother-brother and father-son relationships, with attention to lack of emotional fluency in such familial relationships, arguing that they should too be taken into consideration in any analysis of male homosociality in terms of providing a blueprint for the homosocial relationships that might occur in a man's life. Then the chapter moves to the relationship between Felix and Simon, which is the only positive, meaningful, and discernible example of male homosociality in Rooney's novels. Deploying inclusive masculinity theory, the relationship is examined in light of both the sociocultural conditions that enable it to occur and the possible positive impact it has on Felix and Simon. The chapter invites an expansion of homosociality as a construct that includes all male-male relationships, including kinship structures, and it further encourages more critical attention to positive male homosocial relationships.

The first different kind of relationship between men that is witnessed in *Beautiful World, Where Are You* is the relationship between brothers. The first time Felix's brother is mentioned is halfway through the novel where, after a very long day at work, Felix finds himself seated in his car, rolling a joint, and going through the missed calls and messages he had received while at work. Among others, Felix reads a text message from his brother, Damian, who attempts to organise a meeting between the two so that they can sort out some things, what exactly is not known to the reader at this stage (BWWAY,

DOI: 10.4324/9781032644974-5

p. 167). While reading this message, Felix revisits the entire message thread between the two brothers where it becomes clear that he has been avoiding meeting his brother for some time. 'The previous text was one Felix had sent yesterday, reading: Off work tmr night, will call u. Before that were several missed call notifications from Damian. Ten days previously, a text from Felix read: Hey sorry no im away' (BWWAY, p. 167). Felix dismisses all notifications from Damian and does not call him back or reply to his messages at that moment. Instead, he visits Alice, and later in the night he sends Damian a message explaining that he is not at home but that he might be able to pass by Damian's house the following day. The short exchange that follows reveals that the two brothers are not in close contact with each other, with Felix having been avoiding Damian's texts for three weeks and Damian not knowing where his brother has been or what he has been doing during this time (BWWAY, p. 172). Damian's last text to Felix highlights his disapproval of Felix's behaviour. 'Cop on to yourself Felix. Where are you now that you can't ring me?'(BWWAY, p. 173), he writes, but Felix does not respond. A few weeks later, at Danielle's birthday party, Felix and Alice meet Damian, who is also there, though it is unclear whether he was a party guest or just knew that Felix would be there and decided to go, knowing that he would not be avoiding him if they met face to face in that setting. In that scene, Damian seems determined to ridicule Felix in front of Alice by telling her that Felix cannot read (BWWAY, p. 297). He also explains to her the reason he insists on meeting with Felix.

> See, when our mam died, Damian went on, she left us both the house, yeah? And we agreed we were going to sell it. . . . Anyway, I can't sell it without his signature on all these documents. And in the last few weeks, he's just disappeared. Won't answer my calls, texts, nothing.
>
> (BWWAY, p. 298)

In the remaining part of his stay at the party, Damian continues to belittle Felix to Alice by highlighting how poor and unworthy of her he is. He then leaves when Felix promises to sign the documents the following day. The siblings do not share any other exchanges in the remaining part of the novel, suggesting that it was not only the death of their mother that had a negative impact on their interactions but that they were not in good terms despite her passing.

After Damian goes back into the house, Felix tells Alice that they were never in good terms with one another. He says that their relationship was problematic before the passing of their mother, and he continues explaining that since he was young, Damian would regularly belittle other kids so that he would feel good about himself.

> We hate each other, by the way. . . . We were never great buddies, he added. But the whole thing with Mam getting sick, yeah. . . . But anyway, me and

> him have not been getting on the best in the last few years. . . . He's one of
> these lads who has to put other people down so he can feel like the big man.
>   (BWWAY, pp. 299–130)

According to Felix's account, Damian exemplifies some of the characteristics Messerschmidt (2018, p. 76) ascribes to hegemonic masculinity, namely bullying other men as a way of affirming their dominating position and ascending to a prominent cultural position of power. Such behaviours are exhibited by many of Rooney's characters and have already been discussed in previous chapters. Examples include Jamie in *Normal People* and Derek in *Conversations with Friends*. However, what is interesting about the dynamic between Damian and Felix is that they are not friends or acquaintances; they are brothers. Current scholarship on homosociality does not seem to address brother-brother relationships, as attention seems to be placed on friendship networks between people who are not related through a familial bond. However, the relationship between brothers – and siblings, more generally – is a significant one and warrants some attention in any discussion focusing on homosociality. Buchanan (2021, p. 379) demonstrates the significance siblings may have one another, especially during difficult times when a person might find themselves being able to only turn to a sibling for support. Indeed, recent studies focus on the role of siblings in providing care for brothers or sisters suffering severe mental illness (Kitzmüller, Wiklund Gustin and Kalhovde, 2023) or siblings' experiences when losing a brother or sister of drug-related reasons (Perrin, 2023). The foci of these articles in less quotidian situations highlights a significant gap in the literature. Sociological investigations on the significance of sibling relations such as the work of Davies (2015) and Stocker *et al.* (2020) highlight the probability of a connection between strong sibling relations and overall well-being, but there appears to be little attention to the dynamics between brothers from a masculinity studies perspective. Albeit short, the interactions between Damian and Felix highlight the significant role a brother-brother relationship might play in defining a man's way of navigating other homosocial relationships in their lives. That is to say, it is possible, though speculative, that Felix engages in superficial relations with his male friends because he did not have a more meaningful relation with his brother while growing up. This calls for empirical studies that can examine this appropriately; however, the significance of this familial bond for Felix's development is clearly highlighted in the novel.

Another familial relationship that is illustrated in *Beautiful World, Where Are You* is the one between father and son. A similar relationship was discussed in the second chapter of this book, where the role of the father-son relationship was analysed in relation to the possible ways it may impact the quality of future homosocial relationships for young teenagers as illustrated in *Normal People*. In that chapter, the apparent significance of the father figure as a relatable point of connection among teenage boys was also discussed, examining boys' arrogation of their father's achievements as a way to accumulate social capital and, in turn, assume a dominant position in their relationships with other boys. In *Beautiful World, Where Are you*, we witness the quality of the relationship between Simon and his father through a conversation Simon has with Eileen about it. In this discussion, it emerges that Simon's father appears to be rather antagonistic toward him. As an example, Simon narrates an incident that happened the last time he was at his parents' house whereby Simon had a headache which interfered with his ability to spend quality time with his parents.

> He didn't talk to me all day, and then in the evening he gave me this big long speech about how much my mother had been looking forward to seeing me and how I had ruined her whole weekend by having this headache. He can never say he's angry with me himself, he always has to project his feelings onto Geraldine, like it was a personal insult to her that I had a migraine.
>
> (BWWAY, p. 149)

There are two points of interest in this incident. Firstly, the triggering event that encouraged Simon's father to get angry with his son appears to be not only of minute importance but certainly not a reason to be angry with someone; quite the contrary, one would expect a headache to be a reason of concern and expression of interest from a parent to their child. Secondly, and more relevant to the analysis of male homosociality, the father's apparent inability to direct his emotions toward Simon highlights a lack of affective quality in father-son and, by extension, other male homosocial relationships. The inability of some men to connect to their emotion and/or communicate it to their male peers has been previously discussed in this book. What is of interest through this incident, though, is that it enables a consideration of such inability as a learned behaviour; that is, it portrays the inability of paternal figures to assume ownership of their emotions, no matter how positive or negative they might be, and to communicate them with their children as a possible reason for the consequent inability of their children to engage their affect in their relationships with other men.

Empirical studies confirm the significance of the father-son relationship in relation to all aspects of the son's developmental process, including the son's socialisation into gender and gendered behaviours. Mussen and Distler (1959, p. 355) observe that the father is perceived by the son as the person who is in close proximity, physical and otherwise, to them and knows the most about masculine behaviour. By rewarding gender-appropriate behaviour and punishing gender-inappropriate behaviour, fathers teach their sons how to act as men. It should be noted that the 'teaching' Mussen and Distler (1959) refer to does not have to be explicit. Rather, behaviours that are displayed by the father can be considered gender-appropriate ones, while those which are avoided by the father can be considered gender-inappropriate. As such, observing his father suppressing and/or avoiding showing his emotions might have affected the way Simon handles his own emotional state and, by extension, his emotional and mental well-being. Indeed, Pitsoane and Gasa (2018, p. 10748) provide evidence supporting that one contributing factor to adolescent boys encountering behavioural and emotional difficulties is the presence of tense father-son relationships. The second chapter of this book focuses on this by discussing how, in *Normal People*, Connell and his secondary school peers negotiate their relationships with their fathers (NP, p. 46) and the importance such relationships have in relation to how they negotiate their homosocial relations with their peers. Floyd and Morman (2003, p. 599) also confirm the significance of the father-son relationship, arguing that it is the most important male-male relationship a man will most likely have in their lives, and they highlight the importance of evident expressions of affection, including verbal ones, from the father to the son in establishing and maintaining a positive relation. It appears that a father's ability to be emotionally vulnerable in front of their sons and to discuss their emotions, including but not limited to expressing their love, has a significant contribution to the quality of their relationship with their sons as well as to the son's overall well-being. However, Cleary (2022, p. 11) makes an important point about the subjugation of fathers to hegemonic masculinity and patriarchal ideas about appropriate manly behaviours. That is, men who become fathers are limited by normative masculinity scripts which dictate how they should parent their children. As such, it is important to consider not only how a father's inability to parent affectively might impact their son's sense of gendered self but also how this inability occurred in the first place. Since the father-son relationship adheres to the same regulatory mechanisms as all other male homosocial relationships discussed in this book, it is important, much like the relationship between brothers that is discussed earlier in this chapter, that the father-son relationship is examined from the perspective of male homosociality. Current scholarship focuses primarily on negative effects ineffective fathering can have on children. However, it is important to consider this relationship as a heavily regulated gendered relationship where both parties are constrained by ideas connected to socially accepted forms of masculinity. Further, given that this is the first homosocial relationship men can find themselves in, it is likely that it might affect all future homosocial relationships they might establish and the way they might negotiate these relationships.

Even though it would not be possible, or appropriate for that matter, to assume a causal relationship between Simon's father's inability to emotionally connect with himself and his son and Simon's way of negotiating his own relationships with other people, the novel provides opportunities to witness Simon struggling to establish, let alone maintain, social relationships with other people, especially men. In fact, the only instance where Simon is observed to discuss with another man is while he is on the train with Eileen on their way to meet Alice in Ballina. In her letter to Alice, Eileen explains that Simon 'is currently in a long conversation with some random man I have never seen in my life while I sit here typing this message', and later she explains that the man 'who's talking to Simon is now sitting down at our table and showing him something on his phone. I think it might be a picture of a bird? Maybe the man is some kind of bird enthusiast?' (BWWAY, p. 247). Even though this incident suggests that Simon can easily start a conversation about a random topic with a stranger, this is something that does not occur in any other part of the novel. Arguably, this could suggest Simon's easiness to relate with other men on matters that are superficial, but when it comes to more meaningful, serious relations with other men, he might be less able to establish and maintain such relations. While speculating about the future, Eileen observes, 'Simon will probably continue to be a highly competent and good-natured but emotionally inaccessible person' (BWWAY, p. 248). It emerges that Simon is not significantly different to his own father and seems to be mirroring his father's inability to be emotionally fluent. Whether this is what prevents him from establishing meaningful connections with other men or not is not addressed in the novel, but it can be assumed that it might be one reason for this. Such behaviour seems to be common among all the men in *Beautiful World, Where Are You.* For example, earlier in the novel when Alice visits Felix's house for the first time to meet his friends, Felix and six other male friends of his are not seen to be having any interactions at all except when they check Alice's Wikipedia page to confirm that she is indeed a published author, as Felix introduced her to them. Like Simon, Felix does not seem to be antisocial in that he finds himself in the company of other people, but, also like Simon, he seems to be unable to connect with them at a level that is not superficial. This is not different to the absence of meaningful relationships with other men that Nick from *Conversations with Friends* seems to be experiencing, turning this almost into a motif regarding Rooney's male characters and their lack of emotional fluency in homosocial relations.

At this point, it is important to consider the sociopolitical particularities that contributed to the development of Irish masculinities. Ging (2019, pp. 386–387) argues that contemporary Irish masculinities ought to be understood in light of Ireland's post-colonial nationalistic project. In particular, she explains that following the emasculating discursive practices of the British colonisers, a significant step toward the creation and maintenance of a post-colonial national identity was the rewriting of gendered, and in particular masculine, scripts and the strict adherence to these scripts. The 'new Gaelic man' (Ging, 2019, p. 388) had to be diligent, patriotic, prioritising family, focused on community, and holding strong moral values. The role of the Catholic Church should also be considered, not only as the central pillar of Irish society but also in relation to its contribution to the establishment and promotion of societal definitions of appropriate and acceptable masculine behaviour, including a strict dissociation from feminine traits and a disavowal of homosexuality (Hofstede, 2016, p. 178). For Diamond (2022, p. 33), emotional detachment is viewed as a symptom of an anti-homosexual sentiment nurtured in late nineteenth, early twentieth century Ireland. In particular, Diamond (2022) explains that homosexuality was believed to challenge the integrity of Irish nationhood and, as such, was strictly undesirable. Along with homosexuality, behaviours and traits that were stereotypically associated with it were also rejected. One such trait was emotional fluency, which was considered to be a feminine and, by extension, an effeminate trait. As such, it is very likely that Irish men were socialised into rejecting all connections with their affect, resulting in behaviours such as the one exhibited by Simon's father discussed earlier in this chapter. More recent sociocultural changes appear to have had a positive effect on Irish masculine expectations. Ging (2013, p. 182) argues that contemporary masculinities, at least in the way they are represented in popular culture, provide an optimistic escape from strict heteronormative and patriarchal restrictive scripts whereby the financial prosperity of the Celtic Tiger period allowed for a more cosmopolitan outlook on accepted, if not encouraged, displays of masculinity. That is, the ideal blueprint promoted through popular culture was a new Irish man who was liberated from religious pressures, practised more involved parenthood, was a citizen of the world, and had a stable emotional state. This portrayal was criticised by Ging (2013) as propagating neoliberalism instead of reflecting an accurate depiction of contemporary Irish masculinities. Indeed, post-Celtic Tiger representations of masculinity are less sterilised and illustrating the severe impact of capitalist and nationalist expectations of masculinity on young Irish men (Bollas, 2022, p. 58). It appears that traditional expectations associated with desirable displays of masculinity with regard to emotional fluency are stronger than socioeconomic currents which, in turn, has had an important impact on men who often find themselves unable to connect to and communicate their emotional state, thus affecting the potential for engaging in meaningful relationships with other people, including other men. The regulation of emotion that men are subjected to seems to be a significant contributing factor to reducing the potential of male homosocial relations to be meaningful and beneficial for the men who form part of them. So far in this book, emotional detachment is demonstrated to have affected all types of homosocial relations presented in Rooney's novels: father-son, brother-brother, friend-friend.

Despite the superficiality of many relations between male characters in Rooney's novels, Felix and Simon in *Beautiful World, Where Are You* seem to be establishing a meaningful relationship that provides an optimistic potential about contemporary men and their ability to form meaningful bonds with each other. Even the first time the two men meet each other at Alice's house, it becomes clear that Simon enjoys Felix's company.

> He paid . . . a good deal of attention to Felix, catching his eye now and then and smiling in a vague conspiratorial way, as if pleased by the presence of another man, or pleased by the presence of the women but wanting to share or acknowledge this pleasure with Felix.
>
> (BWWAY, p. 252)

Not only does Simon show that he enjoys Felix's company; the extract is significant because it highlights Simon's need to connect with another man so as to share his excitement with him. This is the first time in all three novels by Sally Rooney under examination in this book where a need of a male character to share an emotional reaction with another male character is presented in such an overt manner. During the rest of the night at Alice's house, the two men do not appear to have many interactions, except when they ask one another about work (BWWAY, pp. 252–253). Even though the topic might appear to be mundane, this is the first time in the novel that Felix appears interested in asking another man a question that will help Felix to get to know the other man better. In all previous interactions Felix has with other men in the novel, he appears either to be completely disengaged (BWWAY, p. 47) or to be discussing topics that are not personal, such as sports (BWWAY, pp. 217–221). A very similar pattern can be observed with Simon, whose only interactions with other men in the novel are limited to being talked down by his father about a political disagreement (BWWAY, p. 149), avoiding interaction with Peter at Leanne's party (BWWAY, p. 198), and engaging in small talk about politics with strangers on his way to meet Alice (BWWAY, p. 247). As such, the fact that Felix and Simon ask one another about their jobs is significant in that it is the first time both men are observed to be interested in getting to know another man, opening up to the possibility of creating a friendly bond with each other.

Haywood *et al.* (2017, p. 67) differentiate between vertical and horizontal male homosociality, arguing that the former refers to homosocial relations that promote a hierarchy imperative of hegemonic masculinity, while the latter describes relations which are founded on emotional proximity, intimacy, and a selfless form of companionship. They further argue that the emergence of horizontal homosociality challenges traditional hegemonic understandings of masculinity resulting in a re-articulation of hegemonic masculinity whereby traits such as engaging in close friendships with other men become desirable and normative. Anderson's (2009, pp. 151–152) empirical research further confirms changes in societal definitions of heterosexuality and male homosocial relations. What is illustrated by Felix and Simon in the exchanges that are discussed earlier in this chapter as well as the ones that are presented in what follows suggests that men's relationships with other men do not have to be superficial, nor do they have to be driven by a desire to dominate one another. The fact that the two men find interest in each other's company and are interested in further exploring this relationship by prompting each other to talk about themselves suggests the need they have to establish such a relationship. Male participants in Grief's (2006, p. 11) study report that friendships with other men are very significant in helping them form a sense. They further report that having someone to listen to them when needed is possibly the most important benefit they gain from their friendships with other men (Grief, 2006, p. 12). These findings are consistent with Botschner's (1996, p. 242) argument regarding the social significance of male friendships in relation to the space they offer for the construction of selfhood as well as to the provision of support in times of need. Indeed, in some of the remaining exchanges between Felix and Simon, it becomes clear that they are in need of understanding their own selves, and they do so when they discuss with each other. That is, rather than observing them contemplating motives of certain behaviours or the way certain incidents make them feel, we see them addressing this issue while talking to one another, as if the emerging friendship between the two provides them with fertile space to engage in self-reflection. Further, the similarities between the two in relation to their tremulous relationship with their families as well as a shared kind of masculinity that is somewhat different to celebrated forms of dominant masculinities seem to be contributing to them bonding quickly and discussing very personal matters with one another. Robinson and Anderson (2022, p. 125) report that the culture of bromance allows for open conversations about profound and troubling personal matters, and genuine peer support is observable among close male friends. However, the interactions between Simon and Felix suggest that honest and vulnerable discussions about personal matters as well as solidarity are not only the benefits of close male friendships but also conditions for such friendships to emerge. The two men in focus engage in such discussions not after having established a long-lasting friendship but immediately as they meet. That is to say that it might be the case that men engage in an assessment of the feasibility of establishing a close friendship with another man early on by prompting discussions that are more personal and meaningful.

The second time Felix and Simon interact with one another is during a beach visit where the two of them, together with Eileen and Alice, spend a day by the sea. The exchanges between the two men almost singularly monopolise the relevant chapter where the beach day is discussed. The two of them appear eager to spend time with and get to know one another. 'Taking his shoes off, Simon said he would go and see what the water was like. Felix, toying with the drawstring on his swimming shorts, smiled to himself. I knew you'd say that, he said. Go on, I'll go with you, why not' (BWWAY, pp. 259–260). Even though Simon does not ask Felix directly to join him for a swim, it is clear from the exchange that he wants Felix to accompany him, and, similarly, Felix seems to have been waiting to spend some time with Simon and seizes the opportunity. Even though the beginning of their conversation is about work, with Felix 'asking what [Simon] actually did all day' and if he is 'renting in Dublin' or not (BWWAY, p. 260), Felix quickly starts telling Simon about his mother's passing, the mortgaged house he and his brother inherited from her, and that they are now in the process of selling the house. Simon expresses his sympathies and asks Felix how he feels about selling the house. This is the first time in all three novels by Sally Rooney where a man is observed to be asking another man about his feelings. Even toward the end of *Normal People* where Connell is very stressed psychologically and mentally, Niall advises him to seek professional help, but he does not overtly ask him how he feels, nor does he encourage him to open up and share his feelings. Simon's prompting Felix to talk about his feelings becomes an opportunity for Felix to explain what has caused the argument between his brother and him.

> I'm avoiding my brother for the last six weeks, trying to get out of signing it over. Isn't that mad? I don't know why I'm doing it. It's not like I want to live there. And I really need the money. But that's me, can't do things the easy way.
>
> (BWWAY, p. 261)

In the moment, Felix appears to be contemplating not only the way he responded to the idea of selling his mother's house but also an overall tendency to complicate matters for himself. Following Felix's lead, Simon also engages in some self-reflection when he responds to Felix commending him for his work with refugees and asylum seekers. He says that he feels 'increasingly frustrated with his work', and he continues saying,

> [m]ost of the time I'm going about my life like it's not even happening. . . . I mean, I meet with these people who've gone through things I can't even begin to understand. And as much as I'm on their side in principle, and I go to work every day and do my job, in reality I spend most of my time thinking about – I don't know.
>
> (BWWAY, p. 261)

What is interesting about the interaction between the two men in this moment is that they are sharing very intimate thoughts and feelings with each other, despite the fact that this is the second time they are interacting, suggesting both that they feel comfortable in each other's company but also, and most importantly, that they had a need to externalise their inner thoughts and feelings.

Indeed, inability to disclose and share emotion can have severe effects on a person's mental and emotional well-being (Pennebaker, Zech and Rimé, 2001). As discussed in the previous chapters, the two main male characters in Rooney's first two books experience mental health issues which were arguably exacerbated by the limited opportunities they had to discuss them with their peers. For example, Nick in *Conversations with Friends* confides to Frances that he often suffers from depressive episodes (CWF, p. 124), but there is no point in the novel where he discusses this in more detail, let alone asks for help. The rare instances where he talks to Derek about an illness of his – not a mental health–related one, Derek downplays the severity of Nick's illness (CWF, p. 98), which can arguably suggest that if Nick were to share his mental health–related issues with Derek, he would downplay the importance of these as well. Similarly, in *Normal People*, Connell finds himself alone in moments that are crucial for his well-being. For example, following the anniversary Mass for Marianne's father, Connell is having drinks with some of his friends. There, he sees his old economics schoolteacher, Miss Neary, who buys everyone shots, and then Connell finds himself in her apartment, not knowing how he got there. Even though very drunk, Connell asks Miss Neary to stop when she unbuttons his jeans and then again when she puts her hand inside his underwear, and he eventually manages to make her stop when he tells her that he is about to get sick (NP, pp. 128–130). The first question that is raised in response to this incident is why Connell's friends let him leave the bar with Miss Neary in the first place. On the one hand, Connell's friends do not seem to protect him by encouraging him to stay with them in the pub, though they might perceive sleeping with a teacher as an achievement deserving celebration; at the same time, the fact that Connell does not have any meaningful connection with any of his friends, especially the ones with whom he is having a drink after the Mass, might have contributed to him deciding to leave the pub with his schoolteacher in that there was nothing important or interesting keeping him there. In the remaining part of *Normal People*, Connell is not seen to discuss his assault with any of his friends, and, given how his mental health becomes worse in the latter part of the novel, the extent to which this incident and the fact that he had nobody to discuss this with contributes to the deterioration of his mental health is unknown. Rentoul and Appleboom (1997, p. 271) confirm that male victims of sexual assault experience severe post-assault trauma which is aggravated when they do not have anyone to confide in regarding the incident and its effects on them. As such, it can be assumed that homosocial relations could have contributed positively to the mental health of both Nick and Connell.

The interaction between Felix and Simon is significantly different to all other instances of male homosociality observed in Rooney's novels. Through their conversation, they continue opening up to one another emotionally. For instance, when Felix asks Simon if he is religious, Simon explains that in the past he considered becoming a priest. Felix asks him why he did not do so, and Simon explains, 'I was going to say that I thought politics would be more practical. But the truth is, I didn't want to be alone' (BWWAY, p. 262). The fact that Simon shares what his original answer would be and what his actual answer is illustrates the level of comfort he must be feeling in Felix's company. It appears as if he has two answers to the question: a rational one, focusing on the practicality of politics, and a more honest one, focusing on his fear of being alone. His vulnerability encourages Felix to also share more personal feelings with Simon. He starts giving advice to Simon by saying, '[y]ou should do what I do, just be a dickhead and enjoy life' (BWWAY, p. 262). When Simon tells him, '[y]ou don't seem like a dickhead' (BWWAY, p. 262), Felix responds, 'I've definitely done a lot of stuff I shouldn't have done. But there's no point crying over it, is there? I mean, maybe I do cry over it sometimes, but I try not to' (BWWAY, p. 262). It is interesting to observe how the dynamic between the two unfolds. It appears almost as if each is waiting for the other to address something more vulnerable or personal for them to follow suit. Without much prompting, they both appear engaged in their conversation. The remaining part of their time at the beach is very similar with them having long conversations while in the sea, talking about Simon's Parisian girlfriend (BWWAY, p. 267), or Eileen and Alice (BWWAY, p. 268). Similarly, after leaving Danielle's party, the two men continue engaging in conversations that are not superficial, such as Simon's relationship with his parents and his insecurities in relation to their expectations of him. He says, 'Whenever I think about my parents I feel guilty. I was just the wrong son for them, it wasn't their fault' (BWWAY, p. 309). Despite the very short time the two men know each other, they appear to connect at a deeper level, such that allows instances such as this one where Simon discusses feeling that he fails his parents' expectations. *Beautiful World, Where Are You* is significant in the way male homosociality is portrayed, especially when compared to the other two novels by Rooney, because it exemplifies the potential for a meaningful connection men can establish with one another and the positive benefits that can come from it.

The relationship between Felix and Simon in *Beautiful World, Where Are You* as well as between Connell and Niall in *Normal People* illustrate Anderson's (2009) the inclusive masculinity theory, which posits cultural intolerance toward homophobia as a catalyst for changing patterns in male homosociality. As per Robinson and Anderson (2022, pp. 79–82), this does not necessarily mean that the men involved in a homosocial relationship do not assume or display any homophobic traits; rather, it refers to an overall social context of intolerance toward homophobia. The rationale is that, in a society where homophobic attitudes are frowned upon, policing gendered behaviours is likely to be less forceful. As such, men might be less likely to monitor their behaviour and, as a result, engage in more meaningful relationships with other men, given that societal definitions and concerns over sexuality and gendered behaviour are less fixed than they used to be. This is perhaps illustrated better in *Beautiful World, Where Are You*, given that the sexuality of the two men is more fluid than heterosexual and homosexual definitions. Felix is openly bisexual, and Simon, although he has not engaged in any sexual and/or romantic relationship with another man, leaves the possibility open.

> Just girls, is it, [Felix] said. Simon looked around at him then. Sorry? he asked. With a serene expression Felix looked back at him. Is it just girls you like, he said. For a moment Simon said nothing, and then in a low easy tone of voice answered: So far.
>
> (BWWAY, p. 269)

In the course of the novel, the relationship between the two men does not appear to involve anything romantic and/or sexual despite the fact that Felix admits to having flirted with Simon (BWWAY, p. 294). In *Normal People*, both Connell and Niall are in heterosexual relationships, without any indication of either of them being interested in exploring different sexualities. However, they never display any homophobic behaviours, nor does the narrative and the characterisation suggest that they could be potentially homophobic. Quite the contrary, they come across as indifferent to the way other people are and behave. Therefore, inclusive masculinity theory could provide an explanation as to why the two pairs of friends are seen to engage in meaningful and supportive homosocial relations. Contrary to *Normal People*, in *Beautiful World, Where Are You*, the relationship between the two men is presented in detail, allowing for a detailed examination of the dynamic between the two men as well as the ways in which they negotiate and establish their relationship. Rooney's latest book posits a challenge to the main argument of this present book in that homosociality appears to be possible. However, it should be noted that, given how rare such a friendship between two men is in relation to all the other male homosocial relations evident in her novels, it makes this an outlier rather than the norm which, in turn, suggests that heteronormative and patriarchal ideas about gender and gendered relations are still prevalent and ought to be challenged. The benefits that close homosocial relationships provide to the men who are engaged in them attest the need for a society that encourages and promotes male homosociality without policing or regulating it.

References

Anderson, E. (2009) *Inclusive masculinities: The changing nature of masculinity*. London: Routledge.

Bollas, A. (2022) 'Normal people (2020) and the new post-Celtic Irish man', *Journal of Popular Film and Television*, 50(2), pp. 50–59. https://doi.org/10.1080/01956051.2022.2033156.

Botschner, J. V. (1996) 'Reconsidering male friendships: A social-developmental perspective', in C. W. Tolman et al. (eds.) *Problems of theoretical psychology*. New York: Captus Press, pp. 242–253.

Buchanan, A. (2021) 'To what extent can we rely on support from our brothers and sisters at different stages in our life span?', in A. Buchanan and A. Rotkirch (eds.) *Brothers and sisters: Sibling relationships across the life course*. Cham: Springer International Publishing, pp. 379–408. https://doi.org/10.1007/978-3-030-55985-4_21.

Cleary, A. (2022) 'Emotional constraint, father-son relationships, and men's wellbeing', *Frontiers in Sociology*, 7. https://doi.org/10.3389/fsoc.2022.868005.

Davies, K. (2015) 'Siblings, stories and the self: The sociological significance of young people's sibling relationships', *Sociology*, 49(4), pp. 679–695. https://doi.org/10.1177/0038038514551091.

Diamond, K. (2022) 'Men, misfits, and martyrs: Oscar Wilde, Roger Casement, and the importance of masculinity to the Irish nationalist movement in the late nineteenth and early twentieth century', *Living Histories: A Past Studies Journal*, 1, pp. 33–40. https://doi.org/10.24908/lhps.v1i1.15428.

Floyd, K. and Morman, M. T. (2003) 'Human affection exchange: II. Affectionate communication in father-son relationships', *The Journal of Social Psychology*, 143(5), pp. 599–612. https://doi.org/10.1080/00224540309598466.

Ging, D. (2013) 'Cool Hibernia: "New men", metrosexuals, Celtic soul and queer fellas', in D. Ging (ed.) *Men and masculinities in Irish cinema*. London: Palgrave Macmillan, pp. 182–207. https://doi.org/10.1057/9781137291936_9.

Ging, D. (2019) 'Gender, sexuality, and Irish film', in J. Hill (ed.) *A companion to British and Irish cinema*. Hoboken: John Wiley & Sons, pp. 386–406. https://doi.org/10.1002/9781118482889.ch21.

Grief, G. L. (2006) 'Male friendships: Implications from research for family therapy', *Family Therapy*, 33(1), pp. 1–15.

Haywood, C., Johansson, T., Hammarén, N., Herz, M. and Ottemo, A. (2017) *The conundrum of masculinity: Hegemony, homosociality, homophobia and heteronormativity*. New York: Routledge.

Hofstede, G. (2016) 'Masculinity at the national cultural level', in Y. J. Wong and S. R. Wester (eds.) *APA handbook of men and masculinities*. Washington, DC: American Psychological Association, pp. 173–186.

Kitzmüller, G., Wiklund Gustin, L. and Kalhovde, A. M. (2023) 'Filling the void: The role of adult siblings caring for a brother or sister with severe mental illness', *Global Qualitative Nursing Research*, 10, pp. 1–15. https://doi.org/10.1177/23333936231162230.

Messerschmidt, J. W. (2018) *Hegemonic masculinity*. London: Rowman & Littlefield.

Mussen, P. and Distler, L. (1959) 'Masculinity, identification, and father-son relationships', *The Journal of Abnormal and Social Psychology*, 59(3), pp. 350–356. https://doi.org/10.1037/h0044529.

Pennebaker, J. W., Zech, E. and Rimé, B. (2001) 'Disclosing and sharing emotion: Psychological, social, and health consequences', in M. S. Stroebe et al. (eds.) *Handbook of bereavement research: Consequences, coping, and care*. Washington, DC: American Psychological Association, pp. 517–543. https://doi.org/10.1037/10436-022.

Perrin, J. (2023) 'Applying three different horizons to understand sibling experiences when the brother or sister dies for a drug-related reason', *The British Journal of Social Work*, pp. 1–16. https://doi.org/10.1093/bjsw/bcad090.

Pitsoane, E. M. and Gasa, V. G. (2018) 'The role of father-son relationship in behavioural and emotional development of adolescent boys', *Gender and Behaviour*, 16(1), pp. 10748–10757. https://doi.org/10.10520/EJC-fcc6ca2da.

Rentoul, L. and Appleboom, N. (1997) 'Understanding the psychological impact of rape and serious sexual assault of men: A literature review', *Journal of Psychiatric and Mental Health Nursing*, 4(4), pp. 267–274. https://doi.org/10.1046/j.1365-2850.1997.00064.x.

Robinson, S. and Anderson, E. (2022) *Bromance: Male friendship, love and sport*. Basingstoke: Palgrave Macmillan.

Rooney, S. (2017) *Conversations with friends*. London: Faber & Faber.

Rooney, S. (2018) *Normal people*. London: Faber & Faber.

Rooney, S. (2021) *Beautiful world, where are you*. London: Faber & Faber.

Stocker, C. M., Gilligan, M., Klopack, E. T., Conger, K. J., Lanthier, R. P., Neppl, T. K., O'Neal, C. W. and Wickrama, K. A. S. (2020) 'Sibling relationships in older adulthood: Links with loneliness and well-being', *Journal of Family Psychology*, 34(2), pp. 175–185. https://doi.org/10.1037/fam0000586.

Conclusion

For the most part, in Sally Rooney's novels, the portrayal of men's relationships is characterised by a notable absence of meaningful connections, showcasing a world where same-sex friendships are scarce. The concept of impossible homosociality was first introduced in the opening chapter, which delved deep into the intricate ways masculine gender expression is influenced and reshaped through interactions among men. The primary focus of the first chapter was on Nick's interactions with other men in *Conversations with Friends*, wherein instances were analysed where men share space but rarely, if ever, engage with each other meaningfully. Similar situations in Rooney's other works, *Normal People* and *Beautiful World, Where Are You*, further reinforce the argument that men hinder the potential for homosocial bonds by suppressing admiration, engaging in superficial relationships, and resorting to public displays of belittlement. The rigid adherence to societal notions of masculinity creates a barrier preventing Rooney's male characters from forming genuine connections with one another. Rooney's exploration of these dynamics sheds light on the complexities and challenges faced by male relationships in developing meaningful bonds. Building on the examination of shallow relationships among men in *Conversations with Friends* and the concept of impossible male homosociality, the second chapter demonstrated how teenage boys learn to conform to societal gender roles, leading to isolation and difficulties in establishing deep connections. The second chapter focused on *Normal People* and Connell's adolescent years, analysing his interactions with fellow teenage boys in high school. It explored how these young boys navigate and define male homosociality during this crucial developmental stage. The interplay of hegemony, masculinities, and homosociality was also focused on in understanding these male-to-male interactions. Additionally, the chapter highlighted the significance of sports-related contexts as safe spaces that allow for public displays of emotional connections among men, emphasising the importance of intimacy for them. In the third chapter, male homosocial relationships in *Normal People* during the characters' adult years at university were examined. Shifting the focus to adulthood provided a more nuanced exploration, revealing how homosocial relationships intersect

DOI: 10.4324/9781032644974-6

with social inequalities and gender hierarchies. Social class and socioeconomic status were addressed for their influence on these dynamics. The chapter also highlighted the potential positive aspects of homosociality for young men, promoting mental and emotional well-being. It explored the notion that male homosocial relationships are more accepted when kept hidden or invisible, whereas public displays of affectionate homosociality are discouraged. The final chapter centred on Rooney's novel *Beautiful World, Where Are You*, offering a closer examination of men's homosocial relationships and their significance. Unlike her previous works, this book dedicates ample time to examine the possibility of homosociality between Felix and Simon, presenting a more optimistic outlook on contemporary masculinities. The lack of emotional fluency in brother-brother and father-son relationships was also discussed. The chapter further explored the relationship between Felix and Simon as the only positive and distinct example of male homosociality in Rooney's novels. Utilising inclusive masculinity theory, it examined the sociocultural conditions that foster such connections and their potential positive impact.

The main question this book aimed to address was the extent to which male homosociality is possible. The literature cited in the book, ranging from theoretical conceptualisations of the term as well as empirical studies, confirms that, for at least the most part of history, men have been forming bonds with one another to the detriment of women and men who do not conform to established or accepted forms of masculine behaviour. Indeed, the book offers illustrations of such instances of male homosociality whereby men establish relationships with other men on the basis of shared misogynistic and homophobic attitudes. However, the extent to which these attitudes are indeed emerging from these men or are thought of as compulsory public displays of certain behaviour is not clear. For example, with reference to *Normal People*, where teenage boys engage in such behaviours, it is not clear whether these boys actually believe that women ought to be objectified and/or degraded publicly. An examination of how male homosociality is organised at this age, offered in Chapter 2, suggests that these boys might engage in such behaviours because they are taught that this is the only way for them to connect with other boys and form some sort of relationships with them. That is, in *lieu of* the possibility of emotional connections, misogyny and homophobia become pretexts for teenage boys to form some sort of connections, albeit superficial ones, with other teenage boys. In either case, these behaviours are not to be justified, but the analysis highlights the need of these boys, no matter how tough they present themselves to be, to engage in homosocial relationships. Similarly, the homosocial relationships that are observed among adult male characters in *Conversations with Friends* and *Normal People*, analysed in Chapters 1 and 3, further confirm that men find themselves rarely, if at all, in relationships with other men which are not based on competition, antagonism, and superficiality. These relationships, no matter how insignificant they appear to be, further highlight the effect socioeconomic characteristics have on how they are organised. Among others, social class and adherence to accepted gender behaviour affect the way male homosocial relationships are negotiated to the extent that they indeed become impossible. The only instances where male characters in Rooney's novels are afforded meaningful relationships with other male characters are between Connell and Niall in *Normal People* and between Simon and Felix in *Beautiful World, Where Are You*. In the case of the former, though, male homosociality appears possible, even if scarce, only when it is not publicly visible. That is, Rooney's second novel presents the two men to be close friends with one another, but without bringing their friendship to the fore in the narrative. In contrast, *Beautiful World, Where Are You* is more generous in the way Simon and Felix's relationship is portrayed, suggesting that when the sociocultural context is less demanding in the way masculine behaviour and expectations are policed, men can engage in male homosocial relationships which, in turn, as the novel shows, benefit positively themselves as well as those around them. In short, the novels highlight the positive effects of male homosociality for those participating in relationships where their behaviours are not scrutinised or challenged for whether they adhere to a societal standard, but they also confirm that the possibility for male homosociality is reversely contingent on the degree of societal policing of masculinity.

Index

Taylor & Francis eBooks

www.taylorfrancis.com

A single destination for eBooks from Taylor & Francis with increased functionality and an improved user experience to meet the needs of our customers.

90,000+ eBooks of award-winning academic content in Humanities, Social Science, Science, Technology, Engineering, and Medical written by a global network of editors and authors.

TAYLOR & FRANCIS EBOOKS OFFERS:

A streamlined experience for our library customers

A single point of discovery for all of our eBook content

Improved search and discovery of content at both book and chapter level

REQUEST A FREE TRIAL
support@taylorfrancis.com

Made in the USA
Monee, IL
07 July 2026

56552422R00046